Titles by *Langaa* RPCIG

Francis B. Nyamnjoh
Stories from Abakwa
Mind Searching
The Disillusioned African
The Convert
Souls Forgotten
Married But Available

Dibussi Tande
No Turning Back. Poems of Freedom 1990-1993

Kangsen Feka Wakai
Fragmented Melodies

Ntemfac Ofege
Namondo, Child of the Water Spirits
Hot Water for the Famous Seven

Emmanuel Fru Doh
Not Yet Damascus
The Fire Within
Africa's Political Wastelands: The Bastardization of Cameroon
Oriki'badan
Wading the Tide

Thomas Jing
Tale of an African Woman

Peter Wuteh Vakunta
Grassfields Stories from Cameroon
Green Rape: Poetry for the Environment
Majunga Tok: Poems in Pidgin English
Cry, My Beloved Africa
No Love Lost
Straddling The Mungo: A Book of Poems in English & French

Ba'bila Mutia
Coils of Mortal Flesh

Kehbuma Langmia
Titabet and the Takumbeng

Victor Elame Musinga
The Barn
The Tragedy of Mr. No Balance

Ngessimo Mathe Mutaka
Building Capacity: Using TEFL and African Languages as Development-oriented Literacy Tools

Milton Krieger
Cameroon's Social Democratic Front: Its History and Prospects as an Opposition Political Party, 1990-2011

Sammy Oke Akombi
The Raped Amulet
The Woman Who Ate Python
Beware the Drives: Book of Verse

Susan Nkwentie Nde
Precipice

Francis B. Nyamnjoh & Richard Fonteh Akum
The Cameroon GCE Crisis: A Test of Anglophone Solidarity

Joyce Ashuntantang & Dibussi Tande
Their Champagne Party Will End! Poems in Honor of Bate Besong

Emmanuel Achu
Disturbing the Peace

Rosemary Ekosso
The House of Falling Women

Peterkins Manyong
God the Politician

George Ngwane
The Power in the Writer: Collected Essays on Culture, Democracy & Development in Africa

John Percival
The 1961 Cameroon Plebiscite: Choice or Betrayal

Albert Azeyeh
Réussite scolaire, faillite sociale : généalogie mentale de la crise de l'Afrique noire francophone

Aloysius Ajab Amin & Jean-Luc Dubois
Croissance et développement au Cameroun :
d'une croissance équilibrée à un développement équitable

Carlson Anyangwe
Imperialistic Politics in Cameroun:
Resistance & the Inception of the Restoration of the Statehood of Southern Cameroons

Bill F. Ndi
K'Cracy, Trees in the Storm and Other Poems

Kathryn Toure, Therese Mungah Shalo Tchombe & Thierry Karsenti
ICT and Changing Mindsets in Education

Charles Alobwed'Epie
The Day God Blinked

G.D. Nyamndi
Babi Yar Symphony
Whether losing, Whether winning
Tussles: Collected Plays

Samuel Ebelle Kingue
Si Dieu était tout un chacun de nous?

Ignasio Malizani Jimu
Urban Appropriation and Transformation : bicycle, taxi and handcart operators in Mzuzu, Malawi

Justice Nyo' Wakai:
Under the Broken Scale of Justice: The Law and My Times

John Eyong Mengot
A Pact of Ages

Ignasio Malizani Jimu
Urban Appropriation and Transformation: Bicycle Taxi and Handcart Operators

Joyce B. Ashuntantang
Landscaping and Coloniality: The Dissemination of Cameroon Anglophone Literature

Jude Fokwang
Mediating Legitimacy: Chieftaincy and Democratisation in Two African Chiefdoms

Michael A. Yanou
Dispossession and Access to Land in South Africa: an African Perspevctive

Tikum Mbah Azonga
Cup Man and Other Stories

John Nkemngong Nkengasong
Letters to Marions (And the Coming Generations)

Amady Aly Dieng
Les étudiants africains et la littérature négro-africaine d'expression française

Tah Asongwed
Born to Rule: Autobiography of a life President

Born to Rule

Autobiography of a Life President

Tah Asongwed

Langaa Research & Publishing CIG
Mankon, Bamenda

Publisher:
Langaa RPCIG
(*Langaa* Research & Publishing Common Initiative Group)
P.O. Box 902 Mankon
Bamenda
North West Region
Cameroon
Langaagrp@gmail.com
www.langaapublisher.com

Distributed outside N. America by African Books Collective
orders@africanbookscollective.com
www.africanbookscollective.com

Distributed in N. America by Michigan State University
Press
msupress@msu.edu
www.msupress.msu.edu

ISBN: 9956-558-42-7

© Tah Asongwed 2009
First published 1993

No part of this publication may be reproduced, stored in a retrieval system, or transmitted, in any form or by any means, electronic, mechanical, photocopying, recording or otherwise, without the prior permission of the publisher.

DISCLAIMER

The names, characters, places and incidents in this book are either the product of the author's imagination or are used fictitiously. Accordingly, any resemblance to actual persons, living or dead, events, or locales is entirely one of incredible coincidence.

With love and affection
To Rosemary and the entire family
and
With reverence and deference
To those the African people put first
But foreign interests put last

Contents

Foreword ix
Preface xxix
Acknowledgements xxxiii

1. Early Childhood 1
2. Education 5
3. Initiation into Politics 7
4. Party Leadership 15
5. Party Convention and my Investiture 25
6. From Pluralism to Single Party 27
7. Appointments in Government 33
8. Policies in Some Key Sectors 41
9. The Debt Problem 95
10. Taxation 103
11. Internal Security 105
12. Plots 106
13. Indoctrination 133
14. Disinformation 135
15. Favouritism and Nepotism 139
16. Tribalism 149
17. Political Prisoners and Human Rights 151
18. Democratization 155
19. Mandzah and Africa in the World 163
20. My Legacy 167
21. Post Scriptum 169

Foreword

When President Wan Nei contacted me to write the foreword for this book, *Born to Rule*, I took it as a singular honour, and welcomed the opportunity as a noble calling for me to manifest to the entire world the solid bonds of friendship that have characterized my relationship with him. I also saw it as an opportunity to extol the ties that bind his country, Mandzah, and mine, the United Conquerors Republic, as our two peoples strive to maintain peace and the triumph of democracy all over the world.

I have read *Born to Rule* thoroughly from page to page and from cover to cover and can affirm that it is a seminal contribution to our collective knowledge of African and world history. It is compellingly incisive, satiric, and tongue-in-cheek and, in some places, trenchantly hard-hitting and humorous in its brutal portrayal of the way Mandzah and, by extension, the African continent, is managed and mismanaged. But that's precisely what truth is all about.

I am not in the least surprised that President Nei would make such a meaningful and scholarly contribution to history. He has been the only president of Mandzah since independence in 1960, and because of his great popularity, his people have continued to present him as the sole candidate for re-election in every presidential election. Needless to say, he has always been democratically elected with at least 99.99% and, sometimes, with more than 100% of the votes cast. In fact, judging from the support he enjoys within his own country and the assistance he receives from the civilized world, there is no doubt that he has many more years before him to continue rendering meritorious service to his country and people. Most of those who started out with him, including some who shot their way to power through the barrel of the gun, have already been dumped in the garbage can of history while he lives on as if by some mythical and mystic power.

With the wind of democracy blowing off the heads of despotic African heads of state, we of the developed world have to put our imagination to work to devise ways and means of helping President Nei to hang in there. He has had a secret agenda for the underdevelopment of his country and for the development of the civilized world since his country achieved independence, and needs more time to implement the far-sighted policies, which have wrought us so much good. The eyes of the Western world are on him to justify the use to which he has put all the assistance he has been receiving and continues to receive.

My country, the United Conquerors Republic, is proud that it has such a steadfast friend and stalwart ally in Africa, a continent that sits at the crossroads of history where communist and socialist rebels used to direct traffic. Thanks to my own president's commitment to the cause of freedom and also to champions of liberty like President Nei, we have not relented in our struggle to make it increasingly difficult for any country in Africa and the Third World to democratically elect a regime of its choice, and get away with it.

Indeed, thanks to allies like President Nei, we have a very robust and thriving arms industry that churns out mass destruction weapons to help us maintain peace and love in the world. In furtherance of our policy of peaceful coexistence with all nations, we have been able to export huge quantities of arms to enable various African and Third World countries to fight one another in order to eradicate the spectre of communism and thus open up trade routes for our products.

My government's commitment to exercising the divine right bestowed on it by history to protect capitalism throughout the world and to find business and job opportunities abroad for our people and the civilized world remains unshakable. We most certainly intend to continue the struggle for a just world order. We might have won the war against communism but we are faced with an equally damning foe: economic stagnation. If it is necessary for us to go to war to maintain our economic strength, so be it. The world is made safe by war in that, in the wake of war, comes prosperity.

The world will remember that last year after the civilized world joined hands to reduce the Ebenebot dictator and despot, Nyam Mbab, to size by bombing his country as well as its military arsenal and nuclear plants – thus ridding society of the threat of nuclear proliferation – the civilized world started jostling for major reconstruction contracts to rebuild the shattered and battered country. This is normal because the spoils of war must be shared, and the more war, the more the spoils, and the more the spoils, the more the prosperity for our industries, and by extension, for our people. Nobody ever goes to war for nothing and we were not going to send our boys into war for nothing.

Our people have always supported our government's decision to go to war anywhere in the world – especially against hapless Third World countries – because they know what war procures to our national treasury and psyche. Our churches pray for us and support our going to war because they too know that wherever we have fought, it has been for the cause of freedom to enable them to win more souls for their founder and, in the process, also make some money. And since freedom is ordained from heaven, we have the sacred duty of imposing it on the world.

We have made it perfectly clear that the world will never be safe and free if every tiny republic – and God knows there are countless such republics – starts manufacturing weapons and acquiring nuclear technology. Not only will the civilized world lose the edge in arms research, technology and sales but its way of life will remain perpetually threatened. Since the fate of the world is in our hands, we have to have a monopoly over nuclear proliferation. We cannot allow some upstart Third World goon masquerading as a popular leader to hold the world to ransom. We are the world.

Some political scientists have wondered whether it would not be in the world's interest for civilized society to wipe out all dictators from the face of the earth. This is an issue that is of paramount concern to our government, and we have been working toward that goal by flexing our military might from time to time to instil fear in the heart of Third World dictators who are not our friends. At any rate, we believe that civilized society would be too bored if dictators didn't hold sway somewhere in the world. Not only do we need someone to bully but we also need the distraction of war and the industry that war generates.

I have known President Nei for the past 11 years. The first time I met him was during an official visit I paid to Mandzah when I led my country's delegation to negotiate, on behalf of the developed countries, the prices of certain commodities the civilized world needed badly for its own development: uranium, diamonds, gold, coffee, rubber, timber, cocoa, etc.

I must say President Nei was most attentive to our pleas for a new economic world order and showed a great understanding of our precarious economic situation. He said it was only fair and normal that since the civilized world colonized Africa in an effort to forcibly plunder its resources and established cash crop plantations to fuel its industries and economies, our people should consider it a patriotic duty to return to Africa from time to time to reap the harvest and bring in the sheaves.

In order to further demonstrate his love for the civilized world which was helping to maintain him in power, President Nei also auctioned off to us his personal collection of gold and diamonds – including the mines – to ensure that after he is gone, we will continue to benefit from his largesse. Since he has whetted our appetite we now have our eyes on his wife's collection and should be sending a high-powered delegation to negotiate a deal with her. We hope she will be as generous as her husband given the wealth her compatriots say she has. The delegation is likely to be led by Steve Mansfield Cook, director of the plunder and exploitation department in our ministry of Third World Affairs (Africa Division).

I should like to acknowledge the sacrifices we know President Nei and his people are making for the development of the civilized world. We, in return, are providing him with all the sophisticated arms we know he needs to stave off any opposition to his regime. Our policy has begun to bear fruit as anyone who watches television can see from the scenes of violent repression of peaceful demonstrations, tribal wars, and sheer suffering that fill our screens daily. The ability of television to capture fine details and to provide live entertainment featuring emaciated children and their parents dropping off and dying on the screen before our very eyes is a prodigious development. Therein lies the beauty of war and television. Everything is live, even death. A few years ago, President Nei once again stretched the helping hand of brotherhood to us. In the heat of our presidential elections, we noticed that our president was sagging in the polls and that he needed an issue around which the people would rally. The president set up an election think-tank to brainstorm on issues, and to make proposals.

The think-tank proposed many things the president could do,

including the adoption of tougher immigration laws to make it impossible for Third World nationals, especially Africans, to emigrate to the United Conquerors Republic, launching war on all Third World countries that compete with us in the manufacture of weapons and nuclear technology, hiring public relations firms to clean up the president's image, and lowering taxes. It was also recommended that the president should undertake a visit abroad to prove to his detractors at home and abroad that he too knows foreign policy and can walk in the shadow of great men.

Our people heartily welcomed the measures we took against Third World nations since these people are more vulnerable to our military might and to blackmail. However, it was felt that the government needed to do more. We needed one major issue that would be the clincher: one that would significantly raise our president's profile. We called on President Nei to give us guidance because of his tremendous experience in the techniques of clinging to power.

President Nei was honest and straightforward. He said, he, unlike our president, was in full control of his people through the elaborate spy network he had established in his country because where two or more of his nationals are gathered in his name, each one shall be a spy. He therefore counselled that we should not do like he was doing because our people wouldn't buy it. He pointed out that he knew us well, and astutely recommended that our president sell the idea of a foreign military adventure to our people as a way of boosting his standing in the polls.

As everyone knows, our people adore and even venerate a macho, sabre-rattling candidate for the presidency. Hence, when our president informed our parliament that our people were sick and tired of living in peace and that they needed to embark on a little adventure by declaring war on someone for the fun of it, our parliamentarians received the news with deafening applause, great relief, and good cheer. In fact, our lawmakers reprimanded our government for having given the world a false sense of security by being too soft and allowing a bunch of Third World leaders to adopt an independent stance in political and economic matters when they should be toeing the line we drew for them in the sand.

The parliamentarians further chided the government for not going to war in a long time. They said because the government had been dragging its feet, Third World people were doing as they pleased on the face of the blessed civilized earth where they don't belong instead of roaming round in the jungle which is their natural habitat. The parliamentarians complained bitterly that the civilized world had already stayed out of war for about five years and that it was the longest time ever in our history that we hadn't kicked anybody in the pants and in the groin. No doubt, they said, our economy was going downhill while the rest of the world was having fun.

The parliamentarians concluded that a responsible United Conquerors Republic government is one that acts fast and responsibly each time the bell of history chimes by inventing an enemy somewhere to fight so as to stoke the flame of our patriotism and to oil our war machine. They said no one in the world cared about the ethics of it, much less about international opinion since the entire world had been forced to accept the fact that the United Conquerors Republic rules the roost. After all, it is generally accepted that we are the spokesman for the Select Security Committee established by the developed countries to determine international behavioural norms for Third World countries and the Native People whose land has become our home.

With such a clear and broad mandate, the coast was clear for our president to find an enemy and potential war victim on whom to stick an accusation that would go down well with our people. Since people and, in general, citizens of the civilized world are neither difficult nor politically discerning, they have entrusted their lives to their government and thus caution anything it does in their name, especially when it concerns Third World-bashing.

It was President Nei, once again, who came to our rescue. Because he knows his Third World colleagues well, we asked him to suggest a most appropriate target for a blistering military attack. President Nei recommended that we attack President Ngup Eboh of Kaikai because he had been trying to convince other African leaders to establish a defence alliance and a common market that would make it impossible for the civilized world to deal with each African country separately and advantageously as it had been doing. We felt it was a brilliant idea. President Nei agreed to allow us use his country as a staging post to attack Ngup Eboh, and also contributed magnanimously in raw cash to my president's campaign fund from the aid money we had just given his country.

We will remain eternally grateful to President Nei and all Mandzahs for their invaluable support to us at all times, especially in times that matter. It is our fervent hope that we will continue to maintain closer and more fraternal ties with Mandzah.

Barely a year ago, our restive farmers clamoured for our president's head because they claimed they couldn't find a market for their produce because cheaper produce from the Third World was competing with theirs. Our friend, President Nei, once again intervened and was instrumental in convincing the African Economic Council to take the bold decision to allow my country to dump its surplus wheat, rice and other products on African countries. This has helped to depress the production of these commodities in Africa and encouraged the outflow of their meagre foreign currency resources toward the developed countries of the civilized world. More importantly, it has tied African countries closer to the apron strings of developed countries because we hold their food lifeline.

A few months ago, one of our most widely circulated tabloids, the Nose Poker, which is known for its salacious articles, published an article that did great damage to our president's image and reputation. The article showed a well-known ravishing and bed-hopping model in the nude who claimed to have spent a few days with our president in his country home when his wife had gone on a private trip abroad.

Because of the uproar and furore caused by the article, our president called up his friend, President Nei, for counsel and, according to some reports, for counselling. President Nei couldn't believe his ears when he heard that the act of sleeping with a woman could be the object of great scandal in the civilized countries, and that people in the United Conquerors Republic would kick up such a storm just because their president had been suspected of sleeping with a woman. President Nei said it was normal practice in Mandzah and Africa for a man and woman to be nude when mating.

Our president, needless to say, was teary-eyed and envious of African presidents who have the right to do anything they want not only with their countries' wealth but also with their female resources. To help our president ride out the scandal, President

Nei immediately despatched one of his most trusted witch doctors to clean up our president's image.

Our president was delighted because he had heard that all African presidents have witch doctors to help maintain them in power although no one could explain why, notwithstanding the support of all these witch doctors, some of the presidents still perished in coups or lost power in the new wave of democratic elections taking place on the continent. Moreover, our president had started to lose faith in his astrologer because all his recent predictions had been false. In fact, from the day our president learned that President Nei's walking stick had been tailor-made for him by his witch doctor to help him remain in power for as long as he wanted, our president started nurturing a secret desire to own one. He therefore saw the coming of the witch doctor as an opportunity for him to own a walking stick made of leopard skin that he could poke at will in the eye of any irreverent demonstrator who came close enough to him.

The witch doctor, a lanky old man wearing nothing but camel skin to hide his bulging manhood, arrived at our presidential mansion disguised as a cleaner to ward off suspicion by the peeping press. He did a few weird things with white bed sheets and cowries and then slit the throat of a white rooster. The blood of the rooster was given to our president to drink and he drank it with relish, smacked his lips, and said he'd never tasted such fruity wine before.

The witch doctor next looked sternly at our president and forbade him to have sex or an affair for a month. Our president was – understandably - very angry because he had been planning a trip to a few African countries where he was hoping to be served young, freshly plucked girls for dessert as was customary. He and the members of his delegation still had sweet memories of their last official visit to Ndapbun where they had a blissfully roaring time.

But then, since misfortunes never come singly, the witch doctor gave firm instructions that after the one-month's abstinence, our president must only sleep with a virgin for another month before indulging in his other fantasies.

Predictably, our president flew into a tidal rage because he knew that finding a virgin in the entire United Conquerors Republic would be like looking for the proverbial five-legged sheep. He prayed the witch doctor to allow him sleep with a married woman or, at worse, with one of the female males that loitered in the neighbourhood of the presidential mansion in the hope that she would be served to some visiting head of state. The witch doctor refused and was immediately deported.

In the light of all the help that the United Conquerors Republic and its allies have been receiving from President Nei, it is only natural that we should stand by him against all odds, especially at this historic moment in his country's history when the opposition parties he authorized-much against his will and ours-want his head. A friend in need is a friend indeed and we have accordingly sent secret service agents from our military corps to train his elite troops and to guard him and his palace.

President Nei has asked me many times in private if we are faithful to our friends, and expressed genuine fears that he too could be 'noriegated'. My response has always been that we of the developed world are as faithful to our friends as politicians can be. President Nei explained that, as a friend, he was very concerned that we had attacked President Ngumba Bamngup of Lewojim in spite of the little favours he had been doing for us such as allowing us to use the Rough Straits to police the Abandoned Ocean, providing jobs for our unemployed experts and technicians, compelling his people to procure all their goods and services from us, and, in short, depending on us entirely for their underdevelopment.

President Nei pointed out that he was afraid that what happened to Bamngup might happen to him someday, especially as we had adopted the policy of 'noriegation', which involves the wanton betrayal of our one time close and faithful Third World friends and intervening to remove them from office whenever we believe their policies threaten our way of life. I explained to president Nei in minute detail that I understood his fears and worries. The truth is that we never act like that without a genuine reason, and the fact of the matter is that, although President Bamngup had indeed been a very good friend of our president or, as we usually say in politics, he had been one of our closest allies, he had started taking the friendship for granted. One shouldn't take anything for granted in politics. We love blacks but politics is not white or black.

When President Mandie of Ewop launched a military attack on President Ebene because The Asses, the Ewop national football team, had lost the Okrika Cup to The Owls of Njimwumu, we supplied Mandie with the sophisticated weapons and logistics he needed to fight against President Ebene and then closed our eyes to his human rights violation antics. We even convinced our allies of the civilized world and the Security Network to consider President Ebene as the aggressor, and they saw with us and ganged up against him. We have to continually bring home the point that aggression by Third World countries doesn't pay.

It was and still is our view that the concept of human rights is not the same for the Third World and us. Accordingly, we accept the principle that since Third world people are already used to tribal wars, suffering and misery, a little oppression and killing will not kill them. It is against this background that we shared military secrets with Mandie, pretended that we didn't know he was engaged in influence peddling and drug trafficking activities, and watched him muzzle the press and coo the opposition. If that is not a sign of friendship, I challenge anyone to tell me what is. But then Mandie took our friendship for granted as I have already said, and felt that he was strong enough to start asserting his country's nationalism.

We have nothing against Third world countries asserting their nationalism as long as it does not interfere with the privileges developed countries have been enjoying as a result of their subjugation of the Third World. We are very nationalistic ourselves and that is why we are fighting for the world to become one large United Conquerors Republic family. Viewed in this light, our nationalism is in the supreme interest of the world.

The message we want to take to all Third World countries is that we are for democracy and for the right of peoples to choose the system of government that most suits their way of life. However, such a system should not, of course, threaten the interests of the free and civilized world which has its own lifestyle and standard of living that it must impose upon the world at all cost.

The old and emerging opposition parties in various Third World countries are made up mostly of a noisy bunch of people trained in our universities. One would therefore have expected that they would stand up and defend the interests of the developed world that trained them. Instead, what do we see and hear? They are talking increasingly and defiantly about diversifying their trading partners and re-negotiating certain agreements that we signed before independence giving us a monopoly over their country's economy and resources.

In the midst of this state of flux, President Nei is one of the few presidents defending the interests of the free and civilized world. He has assured us that we needn't have any fear of him because, as long as he liveth, our economy thriveth. We have the urgent responsibility to stand by him through sanctimonious and highly publicized statements.

President Nei loves us and, in order to cement our relationship, he proposed his wife to me during one of my official visits because, according to Mandzah's traditions and culture, a man must share his most prized possession with his best friend. We of the civilized world have great respect for people's traditions and culture. However, when I politely declined president Nei's offer not because I didn't burn with desire but because it wouldn't sit well with our people back home, President Nei demonstrated a keen sense of understanding and was kind enough to replace her with Mrs. Comfort Dzigwah, his minister of social welfare and wife of Mr. Akwara Dzigwah, Mandzah's most popular industrialist.

From the foregoing, it is evident that I know President Nei well and am thus well placed to review *Born to Rule*. From my vantage point, I see *Born to Rule* as filling a great void in our understanding of Mandzah and, by extension, all African countries since, from my own perspective and our secret service accounts, African countries are the same and behave alike.

This is the first time in history that an African head of state has avoided self-serving rhetoric and admitted that he has not been doing much to develop his country, and that, if anything, he has been working tirelessly to remain in power. President Wan Nei has broken the taboo to write, and to bare his soul.

President Nei could have been hopping around the world like most of his colleagues in the quest for legitimacy or to consult with his bankers, or jet-setting in one of his private planes, sleeping around with international call girls supplied by his hosts, and generally living in the fast lane. He chose instead, out of love for his country, to put his family and friends first.

President Nei has visited many industrialized countries over the past few months to solicit loans to repay those he took last year to open up his village in the jungle and to build a presidential mansion there to welcome visiting heads of state and officials of our lending institutions. We welcome this investment as a significant contribution to the economic development of the great and valiant people of Mandzah. If only other African countries could imitate President Nei, people of the civilized world would not hesitate to pump in much needed resources for the underdevelopment of the continent.

I believe we must give President Nei his due. Too often we mortals do not recognize merit. President Nei has been bold enough to recognize that, since he is unable to take care of his country, he might as well pawn it to interested developed countries and leading financial institutions. These institutions have accordingly taken over Mandzah and are dividing the spoils. Civil servants are being fired so savings on their salaries can be used to repay loans; the major utilities (water, electricity, gas, and telecommunications) are being sold off to foreign multinational corporations in the name of privatisation, etc. We have pumped too much money into Mandzah and cannot continue doing so indefinitely. We need our money back and the only way out is for us to take over all Mandzah state-owned enterprises that can generate funds to repay us.

The government of the United Conquerors Republic, especially the Cabinet Committee on Undercover Activities, a government watchdog that oversees all our covert operations abroad, considers that *Born to Rule* is a trove of invaluable information and policy gems, and that it comes in the nick of time because it had become obvious to us that the manuals prepared by our various ministries on Mandzah and the Third world were in most cases outdated and even inconsistent with our present policy toward Africa. Besides, they no longer reflect a true picture of our government's position on most Third World issues involving our government and our allies. We therefore welcome *Born to Rule* as a great contribution to world political history.

Last year our government contacted a few select universities to honour President Nei with a Doctor of Laws *honoris causa* in Political and Economic Philosophy for his mighty acts and deeds on behalf of the suffering masses of his country and for his attachment to the cause of freedom and liberty. We have since then been flooded with phone calls, faxes and letters from other universities asking us if President Nei still has space behind his name for more degrees and titles.

In fact, my first reaction when I was first contacted to write the foreword for this book was to set up a committee of eminent United Conquerors Republic academics to read the book critically in the light of our relations with President Nei personally and the people of Mandzah in general. We did not want a book to be published that could tarnish our ally's reputation and thus sour the harmonious ties that have been the hallmark of our relations. We had to avoid making the same mistake we made when we allowed Sule Pfumpfum, who is in exile in our country, to write disparaging things about his country's leader, President Torotoro ('Man No Run') or Mbenenoh.

In retaliation for our giving sanctuary to Pfumpfum, President Torotoro held our economy to ransom by placing an embargo on arms purchases from us and threatening to withdraw all his money from our banks. In addition, he kicked out all the experts we had sent to help under develop his country and reneged on his promise to contribute to our president's campaign fund. We do not want to give anyone in Africa the mistaken impression that they can hold us to ransom because it could set a bad precedent.

Many people will recall that late last year President Manam Ndom of Tsugeboh fell out with our government for giving sanctuary to Mr. Gyita Choprun, his former minister of finance, pre-finance, debts and liquidation, who ran away from his country with development aid funds and then wrote a scathing book on President Ndom and members of his Cabinet. We would have been acting out of step with our guidelines if we had sent back Choprun and the money when our aim is to encourage foreign investment. In other words, we would have found it difficult to explain to our parliamentarians that while we welcome African Presidents to re-invest development aid funds in our country in their own names, we do not accept it when it comes form smart civil servants. Money should not have any colour or smell.

In this regard, when President Ndom contacted us to arrest and repatriate Choprun to face trial, we refused on principle because Choprun had, in the meantime, re-invested the funds in our banks in his own name. Like any other country, we too are looking for foreign investors, and our government decided in its ten-year development plan that it would give encouragement and incentives to foreigners, especially African civil servants, who want to re-invest in the United Conquerors Republic most of the development aid funds we give their countries as grants or loans.

In any case, we were forced to ban Choprun's book because it almost jeopardized the excellent relations we have been nurturing with President Ndom and his government since independence. While we acknowledge that Choprun's book was factual, we couldn't allow our personal, trade and political relations with President Ndom to deteriorate just because of a fugitive minister on the run.

I am pleased to say that some of our eminent scholars accepted the national calling of reviewing *Born to Rule* in spite of their busy schedule. They have all confirmed that, unlike some book reviewers and literary critics who don't usually know the subject matter of the book they are reviewing or who, knowing it do not read the entire book, they have, considering the prime importance of *Born to Rule*, read every line of it and recommended it highly. Their assessment is that the book will receive wide acclaim.

These eminent scholars are: Dr. Mary-Magdalene Esther Jupiter, Professor *emeritus* of physical politics and international business ethics, Imperialist College of Economic and Political Domination at the Global University of Hallem; the Reverend Thomas Dubious Faith Scott, holy revealed Messiah and national chairman of the Promised Land Interfaith Mission; Dr. Hope Julius Walker, director of the department of interference and foreign intervention in the ministry of Third World Affairs (Africa Division); Mrs. Gloria Susan Quaker-Oats Smith, chief lobbyist, political and economic affairs division in the Office of the President; Simon Peter Lucifer, director of the Erotica Studio and producer of the box-office films, *The Nullity of Presidents and Presidential Wives In The Nude;* Gregg Pratt Page Sr; well-known trial lawyer who defended the 'Bumptious Trio':Alphonso Martin-Reid Chico, presidential adviser on mafia and criminal affairs; Brutus Sly Jones, alias Field Commander, retired Klan and Front member and now founder of the Imperial Segregation and Ethnic Purity Foundation; and

Patrick G. Hamburger Jr. (formerly Vasiliev Bopov Kapov), former M'Khrussian commissioner for immigration and illegal aliens (Blacks Division) who defected from Kruskou and is now a bona fide citizen of our country. Mr Hamburger Jr. now occupies the position of principal adviser to the Keep Them Out Committee, a non-partisan, non-profit organisation established to advise government on how to stem the tide of Third World vagrants into our country.

I would be remiss if I do not mention the invaluable counsel I received from many of our citizens who want to remain anonymous for obvious reasons. They know themselves. Some of them spent most of their lives in Mandzah exploiting the country and exporting gold, diamonds, timber and other commodities but had to rush back home to the United Conquerors Republic after the depletion of these resources. They can't wait to go elsewhere in the Third World and have been phoning my office daily to find out about new job opening or business prospects abroad. They are, of course, impatient to go on other adventures because they can no longer adapt to our country. Life abroad had been too good to them.

Others went to Mandzah as tourists and after spending a few days there returned as experts with first-hand knowledge of what is happening in Africa as a whole. Without their counsel and testimony, it would have been impossible for me to write the foreword for this book.

I would like to single out two individuals although they want anonymity out of modesty. They are Joyce Stella Shapiro and Pete O'Kay Dammit Brown. These two students ran away from home and dropped out of school for love of tourism and adventure. They have spent the last ten years roaming from country to country and were last sighted in a park in Mandzah last month. While their sleeping bags, cameras and binoculars lay by their side unattended, they hugged, necked and kissed to the great amusement of on looking Mandzah kids and their parents who couldn't understand why two apparently normal human beings from civilized society would close their eyes, lick each other's neck and face all over and then start eating each other's lips.

According to Bill Richard Clayton, United Conquerors Republic ambassador to Mandzah, who invited our two compatriots to lunch and dinner many times, these two students have been more than cultural ambassadors of the United Conquerors Republic. Wherever they went, they kept the flame of patriotism burning by smoking grass and wearing our country's popular national outfit-the fashionable torn and patched blue jeans.

Lastly, there is Daniel McDonald Fries II, political affairs counsellor in our embassy in Mandzah. He has been monitoring events in Mandzah closely and passing on the information to the Central Information Bureau for processing. He is credited with designing the new forms and questionnaires that all Third World nationals wishing to obtain a visa to enter the United Conquerors Republic must complete. The forms are so well designed that our Western allies have contacted our ministry of Foreign affairs to obtain them to adapt to their own situation.

Given the trend of things, all Western countries will soon have more or less similar immigration regulations that completely bar the road to Africans flocking to civilized countries under the guise that they are political refugees when in fact our people know that they are running away from the civil war being fought with the arms we supply the warring factions. The term *deportation* must assume its full meaning.

The forms designed by McDonald Fries II, coupled with the new interview techniques proposed by Max Eckhard Rosenberg, enable our embassy staff throughout the world to be able, at a glance, and without resorting to an interview, to read a visa applicant's mind without even raising their head or looking at the applicant. This should help cut down on embassy staff hours and give our staff abroad much needed time to have a little fun and to make hay while the tropical sun shines.

Special thanks go to Fred Newman Williamson, winner of the coveted International Exotic Prize awarded to a white journalist who has consistently written the most fanciful and farcical account of the kinds of happenings that take place in Third World countries. This is what our television viewers are dying to watch - tribal conflicts, wars, famine, starvation, military coups, natural disasters, religious strife, etc.

Mr. Williamson, correspondent *emeritus* of the Whitewash Times is probably this century's most prolific investigative journalist who had made us more aware of the reasons for coups in Third World countries and the role our government is playing in maintaining the stability of dictatorships. Mr. Williamson has been behind every scoop in the news, and this accounts for the high rating of the ARMS TV news program which he anchors from Irope.

I should add in passing that because of his objective reports, Mr. Williamson has been locked up as a spy in most Third World countries where he went to cover tribal wars and civil unrest. It must be admitted that the sight of suffering and war in strange lands heightens our own sense of invincibility, and strengthens our resolve as a people to fight to ensure that other people continue fighting so that we can sit back, enjoy it, and take pride in our own sense of security.

Indeed, but for the timely intervention of our government, Mr. Williamson would have been killed many times over in many countries. It is imperative that these people understand that they will not be allowed to apply their law of the jungle to our citizens.

In this regard, the heads of state of all the civilized countries have reached a mutual agreement that it is not in their own interest to intervene in any form whatsoever to stop tribal wars, mass killings and genocide in Third World countries not only because the jungle is not an easy place to police but because they don't believe they should be the world's fire brigade putting out fires lit by oppressed people against their authoritarian and dictatorial leaders who are our friends.

Moreover, woe betides any country that messes with the lives of our citizens. To show that we mean business, we cut off military aid to President Nonie after one of our citizens was arrested and tried for drug trafficking in the Republic of Bande. Then when nationwide rioting broke out in the Republic of Kwifon against the tyrannical and authoritarian rule of our ally, General Kasingo, we sent troops to help Kasingo when the rioters assassinated our ambassador.

As I see it, *Born to Rule* is more than just the autobiography of a president. Although what President Nei has written about is certainly not new to us because our secret service agents, our foreign embassy staff, missionaries, businessmen, trade delegations, researchers, foreign correspondents, double agents, and government officials have been saying the same thing for years, this is the first time that a living African president has confirmed it.

Given President Wan Nei's independence, integrity and objectivity, *Born to Rule* has responded to all the key issues that most people have been asking about our policy toward the Third World. We continue to warn our nationals who wish to visit foreign countries to be aware that while the Third world is a gold mine, it is also a minefield. Consequently, while exploiting the gold and the opportunities, our people must tread softly because countries with a semblance of stability are simply wearing a mask. Under the veneer of stability lies a deeply encrusted tradition of donor-funded corruption, nepotism, tribal conflicts, wars, and sheer misery. Lest I be misunderstood, let me make it clear that those of our citizens who have been to Africa know that that part of the world holds much attraction for our people. Apart from dirt-cheap labour, clean air, unpolluted beaches and unfiltered sunlight, The Third World has been able to transform our nationals in whom we had lost hope into instant millionaires over night. If any white man can't make a quick buck in Africa, it means they can't even clean their own behind, to borrow an African saying I heard form President Nei.

In addition to facilitating the exploitation of their countries, president Nei and his African colleagues are very respectful of their foreign friends by whom they swear. This can be seen in part in Mandzah's political landscape which has imposing statues of our nationals whom our people don't care to know because no one knows what good they ever did. Among the statues are those of famous slave traders, missionaries, colonial governors and some of our good-for-nothing presidents who receive only passing mention in our history books. President Nei and his colleagues have a more noble vision of heroism and have named bridges, avenues, streets and buildings after them.

In fact, although *Born to Rule* deals in the main with Mandzah, it should be read against the background of what is happening in other parts of Africa and the Third World. It is in the same mould as some of the existing field manuals prepared by some of our ministries for their staff.

For example, *How to survive in the jungle* by the ministry of pollution and the environment; *Field Workers Manual* by the department of disaster forecasting and emergency aid of the ministry of war planning and arms sales; *Third World Guide* by the

Federation of United Conquerors Businessmen; *Handbook for Collective Survival Abroad* by the Presidential Task Force on the Protection of United Conquerors Interests Abroad; *Travellers Vade Mecum* by the National Association of Private and Independent Exploiters; and *World Global Watchdog* by the Consortium of Hallelujah Revived Interdenominational Churches and Reformed Televangelists, Inc. The great merit of *Born to Rule* lies in the fact that it is based on hard facts and not on legends or fiction. It will be found useful by all segments of the population and especially by all Tubab nationals visiting Mandzah and Africa. Also, leaders of the civilized world are likely to learn something from it about how to stay in power. Some of the techniques described by President Nei are well know to us although we haven't yet attained the same degree of sophistication;

There is a crucial omission in Born to Rule, however. One would have expected that President Nei would dwell on the state-of-the-art technological advances the developed and civilized world is making in the fields of violence, in general, and murder, in particular (including mass and serial murder), as well as in racial discrimination, abortion, child abuse, armed robbery, corruption, cultism, etc. Maybe the author didn't feel compelled to go into the details of these topics because all African countries are already making tremendous strides in these areas as compared to other sectors of their underdevelopment. It is to be regretted that the book is silent in these crucial areas that map the civilized world out as a chosen people to lead the world.

The sections in *Born to Rule* dealing with politicians, government officials, disinformation, official government policy in different sectors, etc. have a universal ring. Clearly, there is something for everyone in *Born to Rule* and I strongly recommend it as required reading material to anyone interested in knowing how and why the Third World is spinning round in circles.

> DR. GEORGE STANLEY PETER, JR
> Former Minister of Third World Affairs
> United Conquerors Republic

Preface

It seems incredible to me that so many president-monarchs like me should be passing away without leaving anything in writing to posterity. This is another area in which we on this African continent have shown great bankruptcy. I don't mean financial bankruptcy because we are supposed to have stashed away in our personal national bank accounts abroad enough of our countries' financial resources to live very happily ever after. In this context, I mean political bankruptcy because we know that each time we fire our ministers or accuse them rightly or wrongly (though wrongly most of the time) of fomenting a coup, they become disgruntled and write all sorts if irreparably damaging things about us.

We all know that even in the United Conquerors Republic, there is a kiss-and-tell virus going all over the place, and sooner or later it will reach us like all viruses that are born there. The only way for us to control it is by setting the records straight, and that means we must write ourselves. One only has to read some of the books that have been published in recent times to grasp the urgency of the situation.

I suppose we have all read *Foreign Policy: the triumph of adventurism* by Edmund Dwight Greenberg, former Minister of Foreign Matters under President John Wright Wenger ('The Bullet') of the Hegemony Republic. The book narrates in slurry detail President Wenger's trysts with prostitutes as well as his sleazy connections with the underworld. Who of us wants such revelations? We have a duty to posterity to contribute to the building of our nations by ensuring that the course of history we have charted is not changed. A lot is at stake, and we can't allow other people to write for us nor expect them to forge our history in our place. They will falsify the facts. It is for this reason that I have, in my infinite wisdom, decided to pen down some of my thoughts, debunking the derogatory things prevalent in the world press about my country and me.

In doing this, I am not unaware of the fact that most of us leading Africa cannot even write or read well. But then that should not be an excuse because we are not alone. In fact, we in Africa are in cosy company. One only has to look at all the so-called developed countries which claim to be the custodians of world wisdom to see who is at the helm of their ship of state. A cursory glance at the beaten path of world history shows that intelligent people throughout the world owe so much to so few of us.

I know that each time my colleagues and I meet at our annual Solidarity Meeting and I open my mouth to speak, my colleagues always laugh at me in their handkerchiefs because they say I don't know how to speak and write English well. They think I do not notice them when they are laughing. They may laugh themselves hoarse if they like, but then in fairness to their people, I think they should open their hearts and clear their conscience to history as I have done in this book otherwise after we are gone, everything we have fought for will be dismantled.

It is true that there have been attempts, albeit timid attempts, by some of us to have our memoirs and autobiographies written. In almost all the cases I know, these have not really been memoirs or autobiographies in the sense of the word but a collection of ghostwritten speeches. This may be understandable because a president who takes his work seriously- like we all do- does not have the time to attend to matters of state and at the same time indulge in writing fabricated stories. I suppose that the time we spend formulating the strategies needed to maintain us in power - so that we can finish the national duty thrust upon us by history - is much too short to allow for any other pastime.

To prove what I am saying, I refer the reader to some of the works published on behalf of some of my colleagues: *The Divine Right of African Presidents* by His Royal Oneness, President-for-life, Dr. Prof. Judas Iscariot Ndon; *Chieftaincy and Presidential Politics: A Study in Contrast* by His Excellency, Field Marshall Corinthian Korokoro; *Democracy and Autocracy: Survival of the Richest* by the Reverend Revelation Lolo of the Lolo & Co. Church.

There is no doubt that it is in our own interest and that of our people to set the record straight. I have decided to take the lead and to draw from the depths of my own wisdom.

During the more than thirty years or so that I have been in the driver's seat on the cobbled road leading my country from underdevelopment to underdevelopment, I have spared no efforts in putting my country and my people first. In saying this, I know that some malicious individuals bent on sowing seeds of discord among my people have spread word around the world that I put the army first above all else to guarantee my stranglehold on the people. Nothing could be further from the truth, and I leave it to the reader and history to pass judgement on the sacrificial services I have been rendering my country.

Furthermore, in deciding to write this story about my life as president, I know I am gambling with the political life of my country. I know that the Western press, those information birds of prey and their hired spies, are only waiting for an opportunity like this to launch their smear campaign against me. But then I fear no evil because I walk in the path of righteousness. I take the readers of this book to witness. It is always easy to criticize, but when it comes to making concrete suggestions for change, the vociferous press loses its voice.

Finally, I vowed to myself when I set out to write this book that I would tell the truth and nothing but the truth; that I would call a spade a spade and tell the world what I know about the major events that have shaped the history of my country. I stand by that vow because I have to be true to myself.

After more than 30 years in power at the head of one of the poorest countries on earth, my people and the world must hear from me first-hand about the policies my enemies say I have been adopting to maintain my country in a permanent state of disrepair and bemused underdevelopment.

I hope my colleagues throughout Africa will follow in my footsteps and write their own memoirs and autobiographies to put to rest once and for all the vicious things that people have been saying about our reign. This is a national imperative especially at this time of rapid changes. Who knows tomorrow?

WAN NEI

Acknowledgements

In writing this book, *Born to Rule*, I am indebted to a number of individuals and corporations who, on hearing that I was planning to write my life story, gave me much moral and financial encouragement. First, the Alibaba Association, the umbrella organization of foreign businessmen operating in Mandzah. As it always does whenever a major underdevelopment project is announced, it made a donation of 50 million Francs to my book project, and following the gesture, there was a nationwide outpouring of financial and moral support for the venture.

The Association of Mandzah Newspaper Editors contacted me to give them the right to serialize this book which I refused since I had already promised to give the exclusive rights to a United Conquerors Republic Publisher.

I need not mention the offers I received from major publishing houses in Irope, Hapon, and Criton to publish the manuscript. We have so far collected 130 million Francs, and I am sure that by the time we are through with the collection campaign, we will have collected much more. I take this opportunity to encourage our people as well as our foreign friends and partners to contribute to this worthy cause.

Secondly there is Pius Fon, my minister of information, disinformation, propaganda, and censorship. He did everything possible to convince me to allow him write this book in my name but I refused because I believe I am sufficiently intelligent to write my own life story myself. I am not like presidents of some civilized countries who have to hire people to remember things for them. I felt I should write this story myself because there are too many things that the world press has cooked up in the past against my people and me. I think it is only fair for the world to hear my own side of the story. I believe the world has a right to know the workings of the machinery of a president's mind.

I would also like to thank Alhaji Pepe, minister of education, illiteracy and re-education as well as the dean of the Faculty of Indo-European Languages, Classical Studies and Dead Languages of our National University, Dr. Prof. Kalekale Yayuh who suggested that I remove all the swear words and expletives contained in the original version. He explained that since my book is not a transcription of the Wawagate Tapes that did in one civilized country's president, who was involved in dirty tricks, there was no need for me to be vulgar and crude.

As concerns the political content of the book, I owe an immense debt of gratitude to Dr. Barnabas Moses Tsek, my adviser on domestic and international affairs. No one could have been better prepared for such a national assignment than Dr. Tsek who has extensive experience in the field of common sense and conventional wisdom. In fact, I was the one who wrote the foreword to Dr. Tsek's popular book, *Political Sense and Economic Cents: Unraveling the Nonsense*.

It was Dr. Tsek who, in consort with the United Conquerors Republic ambassador accredited to my country, convinced Habdard University that I, more than most of my colleagues, deserved a Doctor of Laws *honoris causa*. I mention this in passing to clear the air once and for all because I have read snide comments in local newspapers about the way I was chosen to receive the free degree. If anyone deserves it, I think I deserve it even more given my impeccable political credentials.

I have made an outstanding contribution to the arts and sciences of my country. As president of Mandzah since independence, I have brushed aside several fake, imagined and real coup attempts and given real meaning to the concepts patronage, clientelism and personal rule. While my country wallowed in economic crisis, I created job opportunities for my friends, relatives and tribesmen.

Furthermore, unlike my colleagues who have had to lead unstable governments, I have, as a political visionary, used thee armed forces well to monopolize and centralize power, embark on self-aggrandizement projects with the counsel and approval of donors and international finance institutions. I have encouraged the press to promote a sustained and sustainable policy of hero-worship and sycophancy, and eliminated enemies as well as constitutional checks and balances. But while I have amassed power and ruled alone, I cannot claim to have written this book alone without much help. I don't want to lie.

I am carrying the debt burden of thanks owed to too many other people. I would like to thank Julia Green, my devoted secretary for over twenty years. Many people have speculated over the years why I chose a white woman as my private secretary, but those who know Africa well enough don't ask such questions. Those who know Julia closely know that I couldn't have chosen a better person. I don't care what people have been saying about Julia and I, especially those who link us sentimentally. The truth is that I have known Julia since childhood when I was living on the mission with some white missionaries. Julia was the daughter of one of the missionaries, and we became very good friends. A president needs a secretary he can trust; one who can keep matters of state confidential. I believe that Julia has all the virtues of such a secretary.

Julia knows me well and handled the national assignment of transcribing this text beautifully after I dictated it to her at odd moments in the dead of night and sometimes in the contemplative early morning.

Let me now thank members of my family for all the deprivations they have been subjected to by virtue of their being members of my family, and for their help in carrying with me, on our fragile shoulders, the heavy load of responsibilities that go with the presidency. Without their genuine help, especially that of my darling wife whom the nation, in recognition of her sacrificial services, has affectionately called the Mother Teresa of Mandzah because of her good deeds on behalf of the suffering masses of my country, Mandzah would have been torn to pieces by civil strife and general instability. Thanks to my family, this country is considered a bastion of stability and progress on a continent rife with discord, wars, poverty and misery.

Do not mind that the press always unearths from the fertile recesses of its own imagination falsehoods about my having girlfriends strewn all over the country. I debunk all these accusations in lavish detail later on. Breathes there a man with penis so dead that he has never lusted after a woman?

In conclusion, I would also like to say what many writers usually say when they have written something that they know full well to be especially stupid. They usually say that notwithstanding the tremendous help they got from various quarters, they are ultimately responsible for any errors that might have found their way into the book. I would like to say the same thing.

Finally, this autobiography is a historical and political treatise that I am dedicating to our national party, the Mandzah People's Union Party (MAPU) which has, since I founded it, had the foresight to continue imposing me as the sole candidate for election to the presidency of this country. I owe my unbroken string of seven five-year terms of office to it. As we are being forced by the buffeting storms of democracy to share power, I hope the party will remember that I am its architect and that the people of this country owe their station in life to me.

It is gratifying to note that at the last convention, our party took the resolutely bold step of acknowledging the bankruptcy of opposition ideas and elected me Life-President of Mandzah. We have always said we stand for democracy and that we respect the people's will. The voice of the people, they say, is the voice of God. I have already accepted that singular honour and want this book to be my testimonial of appreciation to the people of this country for putting their faith in the institutions that I set up to run down this country so efficiently.

WAN NEI

1

Early Childhood

Many authors have written various things about my early childhood. While some of the things border on truths, half-truths, hearsay, gossip, innuendoes, and so on and so forth, some are deliberate lies intended to seek my downfall from power and to discredit the popular people's movement that I am leading.

I am happy to say that none of these destabilizing acts has succeeded. This is, of course, because I have the people on my side. More important, my power comes from God and no connivance by any wayward group of individuals will deter me from seeking the welfare of my people and my own survival as the shrewd politician and wise leader that people all over the world say I am.

That historians, political scientists, sociologists, anthropologists, psychologists, psychiatrists, the church, the press and others should be so interested in writing about me and my country is evidence that my country is indeed in the limelight of the world. We are flattered.

It is true that I am a bastard as some people have written. I was born around the time of World War I by a wonderful mother whom I never got to know. In fact, I was raised by my aunt, Mrs. Afor Njimtah, and did not know that she was not my real mother until I was about 15 years old. It happened by chance. A classmate of mine with whom I fought and whom I beat to pulp for making fun of my unkempt hair and jigger toes, abused me that I was a bastard. When I returned home later that evening and confronted my aunt and her husband, they confirmed that my mother and my father had met in a bar and that I had been conceived that same night. My father never showed up again, and when my mother delivered me, she could not stand the shame, and so she committed suicide.

I wish to say here that I am not ashamed of my status. Our society should rather be ashamed of the way it treats it unwed mothers for it was our society that drove my poor, innocent mother, then a young and tender school girl, to kill herself. Had my mother done the abominable thing by causing abortion, I leave it to the reader's imagination to fathom what opportunity this country would have missed to have me as their God-given president.

However, it is definitely not true that my security agents arrested, tortured, and later on hanged the editor of the *Mandzah Drum* for publishing a derogatory article about my status. We in this country have a free press and if I had thought that the article in question injured my reputation, I would have sued the newspaper for libel. As to the actual cause of the death of Chicha Chachi whose pen flowed with venom and invective for the government, my country, and me, all I can say is that investigations have been going on for the last 5 years or so to identify the killers or hired assassins.

It is true that we have many journalists in jail, but it is not because they publish false rumors about my status. If we routinely jail our journalists, it is because they recklessly publish inflammatory literature which could incite our people to civil disobedience and rioting.

Let me make it perfectly clear that we in this government are just as surprised as the public about the manner in which Chicha Chachi died. We understand that an autopsy report states that he died of a heart attack. We believe that to be highly probable because the poor chap's heart could not keep on lying as he had been doing. In any case, we are impatiently waiting for the results of the investigation we ordered years ago.

It is also true that when I learned that I was a bastard, I became, understandably, at that young age, very miserable. I could not understand why my father would shirk his responsibilities, but then I have grown to understand that not all men are men. One only has to look at some of my ministers and government officials. They run away from taking decisions and assuming their responsibilities and when the press accuses them of irresponsibility, they say they haven't received instructions from the president's office to do so and so. But then when I give them instructions, they say I am a dictator. I challenge anybody who thinks he is bold enough to look at me in the face and say I am a dictator.

When I was 17 years old, my aunt and uncle decided to send me to live with some missionary friends in Njingyi where I attended secondary and high school. It was on that mission that I met Julia Green, a particularly pretty and wholesome white woman who was later on to become my private confidential secretary. Julia at the time had all the trappings of a princess but decided to hang out with my friends and me.

In those days a student growing up with missionaries was very privileged. There was always good food to eat, good drinking water, a car to take one places, etc. It is obvious that the five years I spent at the mission changed my outlook on life substantially. At that time, I put God first above all else in my life until I realized the power of money and the power of power. It is therefore not for nothing that I am still in full control of my country at a time when many of the colleagues with whom I started in the early 1960s have fallen by the wayside. Even those who seized power later have come and gone while I am still around. In my case, unlike many kids my age, money did not mean much to me, and still doesn't up to this day, as anyone who knows me well can testify. I am not greedy nor have I amassed wealth of the kind the opposition has been trumpeting all over the world.

What in fact did I have that the opposition should be so vociferous about? After being in office at the time for 2 years, I realized that I needed two small castles in Prance (I could have built the castles in the air and nobody would know about them, but I chose to build them on land), an international golf course and a cocoa plantation in my village, a private hospital in Arimeka, and shares in a few international banks. If people think that's a lot, all they have to do is look at what some of my colleagues own just after a few months in power. I want the world to be my witness because this is what I was being crucified for at that time. For Christ's sake, let's not be petty. Although my wife is far richer than I, I am not complaining.

Furthermore, I grew up considering all human beings irrespective of their ethnic origin and skin colour as my kith and kin. This is the vision of life I have brought to public office. Those who know me well know this well. It is for this reason that, as a citizen of this our one world, I have felt free to recruit my security agents and many of our best advisers from Ikrael, Krussia, Arimeka, and Prance. I have not left out any major country because I think my national cake should go round. Indeed, the relative peace and stability my country has been enjoying as a result of my longevity in office, as well as the failure of our economic, social and cultural programs are a direct result of my openness to the rest of the world and adoption of short-sighted policies.

2

Education

I have a very humble academic background and I am proud of it. Although I had opportunities to pursue my studies abroad, especially as the missionaries with whom I was staying were prepared to sponsor me, I decided to stay and militate for my people. My stay with the missionaries had opened my eyes wide to see many things which my fellow countrymen could not see. I witnessed, for example, the daily humiliation to which our people were subjected because they were illiterate.

Let's face it. It is not because someone cannot read and write that he or she is not intelligent just as it isn't because one cannot spell *potato* that one can't be vice-president of the most powerful country on earth. And it is not because one is black that one is automatically more prone to sinning. It was for these and other cogent reasons that I rebelled and joined the patriotic forces that were being formed to obtain our independence.

So much has been read into my disagreement with my missionary guardians at the time that I believe I should shed some light on what really happened. We all know that before missionaries came to Africa, we Africans had our own forms of worship, and still do to this day. I refused to accept the fact that the few Mandzahs that were ordained at the time in the Christian ministry should be housed in different residential areas, cut off from where their foreign missionary brethren were staying.

Yet another thing that really chilled me was the fact that during my entire stay on the mission, I never ate with the children of my missionary guardians. I was always served alone and I would sit in the kitchen and have no one to play with while their children sat in the parlour with their parents. I slowly came to realize that my missionary guardians hadn't really adopted me as their own child as they made everyone who visited us believe.

One day I decided that enough was enough and left. My sudden departure meant that I had to disrupt my studies because the missionaries refused to continue paying my fees. I had already finished secondary school and had begun the first term in high school. Like all children at the time, I began keeping bad company. We would steal food from the market to eat, push trucks, gamble, and sleep in market stalls.

It was at this time that the late Efon Akum scoured the countryside preaching trade unionism. I remember attending some of his rallies where he would call on all Mandzahs to fight for their rights. He referred, in particular, to those Mandzahs who had fought in World War I and who had been abandoned when the War ended without any benefits. Some of these people had lost their eyes, arms, feet, etc. and the colonial government had not given them the care they deserved.

I remember seeing some of these people Efon Akum displayed at his rallies, and to this day, that experience has left a scar on me.

3

Initiation into Politics

I think it is unfair for people to call the organization set up by the late Efon Akum a political party as the colonial administration trumpeted it all over the world. Many people have said it was a hotbed for political activists of the time and that it was something like a nursery for budding politicians. In all fairness to Efon Akum, whom I got to know very well, I must say that he never intended to form a political party. His Mandzah Workers Union was a loose assemblage of workers and non-workers established to strengthen the position of the few workers at the time in salary negotiations with their white masters.

Members of the trade union at the time were nationalists who loved their country and accepted to work selflessly in the interest of workers. But what do we see today? Mr. Shidong, the so-called leader of the Mandzah Workers Union (MAWU), has been running round the country calling on members of the Union to go on a nation-wide strike to protest against the government just because we owe them a few months in back pay. Although I have explained that I am not responsible for the structural adjustment programme that requires us to lay off workers and cut down on salaries, Shidong and his unpatriotic union don't want to listen. They assert that unless I am willing to reduce my own lifestyle and that of my ministers and cronies, MAWU will not allow its members to adjust anything. I don't think the Union is being fair to the country.

In my case, as expected, when Efon Akum started MAWU, the white establishment immediately panicked as it does even today whenever black people band together for any purpose. They called Efon Akum a rebel, a reactionary, and did everything possible to discredit not only the movement but also his family. Efon Akum stood his ground with the support of his followers.

One thing I must say that saved Efon Akum initially was the outbreak of World War II. The white establishment was watching to see if we would enlist in the army to fight against Hitler's Germany as the patriots we had said we were. If we did not, we would be portrayed as enemies of the country, and if we did, we would be served first as fodder for the enemy's cannon. This did not deter us.

We believed that we should pay any price to serve the cause of justice and freedom. Most of the leaders of the Workers Union joined the army and fought valiantly. Some of them were killed and others were maimed, but there were no regrets about their participation in the struggle for freedom. Freedom always has to be won at a price.

After the war, some of the key survivors, including Efon Akum, set out to reorganize the Union. The white establishment, which had thought the movement dead, raised an alarm. Efon Akum and his very lose associates were refused their war benefits and branded as Nazi sympathizers although they had fought on the side of the Allies. The Union tried to organize civil disorder and was crushed. Efon Akum was arrested, and has not been heard from to this day.

Following Efon Akum's disappearance, there was a power vacuum in the Union. Members jostled for power, and soon there was a split in the leadership. Some people preferred cohabitation with the white establishment while others wanted the Union to be transformed immediately into a political party to oppose the stranglehold of the white establishment on the country.

I was one of those who opted for cohabitation. It was my view then that just as the Romance Republic had done during World War II when the Nazis had overrun it, we should, while cohabiting with the white establishment, plan to organize a resistance movement. I did not believe that standing up at that time to the white establishment, which had all the resources at its disposal to crush us, would serve any useful purpose.

It is to be regretted that we did not have a united front in the country because there were now two bitterly opposing factions. Because the Mandzah Peoples Movement (MAPEM) seemed to be more vociferous, the white establishment loathed it and preferred our Mandzah Workers Union (MAWU). As experience from all parts of the world showed, the colonial administration preferred submissive black people who did not clamour for their rights, because a black man is not supposed to enjoy them. The colonial administration alone was supposed to decide what to offer as platitudes to my country.

In the face of the administration's intransigence in giving the black man his due, the movement initially started by Efon Akum (the Mandzah Workers Union) was transformed into the Mandzah Independence Party (MIP). Those of us who refused to champion the cause of independence at the time because we felt we were not yet ready for it broke away and formed the Mandzah Peoples Union (MAPU).

Our refusal to accept independence on a platter was based on our genuine view that independence obtained without a struggle is not independence and that we would be independent in name alone and still depend for everything on our colonial masters. We had neither the trained manpower to man the government and the private sector nor politicians shrewd enough to meet their white counterparts head on in any discussion. The result is that we were given our independence but we continue to this day to depend on the white man.

I recall that one day when the early rains had just set in, one of the missionaries I had known, Rev. Jerry Dogood, came to see me. He sat down on my creaking wooden chair and while gulping down glasses of palm wine and chewing on kola nuts, told me that he had been sent by the white man governor, Mr. Peter John Wilson, to tell me that the white community had decided to support me for the leadership of MAPU.

I told Rev. Dogood quite honestly that I did not feel qualified to be a candidate for the leadership of the party and that our leader, Mr. Isaiah Bonu was, as far as I knew, a very competent leader that was loved by each one of us. I remember even alluding to the fact that Mr. Bonu was a newly converted Christian who had been baptized just a few months earlier by Rev. Dogood himself.

I recall very vividly that Rev. Dogood smiled. He said, using biblical language that I cannot forget, that it was probably God calling me to lead my people from the wilderness of despair and despondency to the promised land of independence. I took a deep breath, and saw parallels between what Rev. Dogood had just said with what I had learned about the story of Moses in the Bible. I asked myself if it meant that God was now choosing me, through Rev. Dogood, to serve my people.

I knew I had neither the training nor the disposition to become the leader of such a valiant people that had contributed to the elimination of one of the greatest scourges of mankind, Nazism. All the same, I thanked Rev. Dogood, and told him that I would think about what he had said, and then discuss it with members of the Executive Board of the MAPU.

Rev. Dogood looked at me in the eye and, while bidding me good-bye, whispered softly into my ear that I should keep what he had told me to myself because the other MAPU members would kill me out of jealousy if they got wind of the fact that the white establishment was grooming me to be a candidate for the leadership of the party.

I gave serious thought to what Rev. Dogood told me, and tried as hard as possible to keep it to myself. It was very difficult for me to be carrying the weight of such information around without sharing it. Slowly, I realized that maybe Rev. Dogood was right to ask me not to divulge such information.

Two weeks after our first meeting, Rev. Dogood returned to see me. He was clutching a big package under the gown that only true reverends are supposed to wear, but that many a man today have started wearing. He said he was in a hurry and that the governor had sent him to find out if I had made up my mind. I replied that I hadn't. Rev. Dogood's eyes drooped. When he raised his head, I could see a little anger jutting from behind his eye sockets. He explained to me that the future of Mandzah lay in my hands and that the entire white establishment had considered me more fitting to deliver my people because the rhetoric of the MIP was blatantly anti-white. He then enumerated the good things all the white people had done for us and said we would lose everything if the MIP took over. He mentioned the good news that white missionaries were preaching and how those of us that believed in the message of salvation would be saved. He also referred to the schools, roads and plantations opened in the country.

Having said this, and while I watched him, he gave me the package. I opened it in front of him, and lo and behold, it contained bundles of money. He said that was part of the white establishment's contribution to help me run my campaign and that more would be forthcoming depending on how I cooperated with them.

It is important that I go into these lavish details because some people have misrepresented my motives for seeking the political kingdom through leadership of the MAPU.

It is true that after listening to the arguments advanced by Rev. Dogood and the other members of the white establishment who had been delegated to convince me to accept such a national assignment, I started becoming attracted by the lure of money. At that point, it wasn't power I was interested in. In fact, power didn't mean anything to me then because I hadn't yet understood the power of power. It started dawning on me gradually, however, that money could resolve many problems.

Before I go on, let me be blunt and state categorically that it is definitely not true that Rev. Dogood promised me military assistance in crushing the MIP which was, to be honest, more popular than our own party, the MAPU. To be candid, people were attracted to the MIP more than to us because they wanted independence immediately whereas we in the MAPU preached moderation and cohabitation. It must be said that the exactions of the white man on the blacks did not help the cause of our party because people failed to understand how we could claim to be patriots and at the same time support the white establishment in the face of all the atrocities it had wrought on our people throughout history.

Given the tremendous pressure to which the white establishment subjected me, I took an appointment to meet with the governor in his mansion. When I met him, he explained to me the sweetness of power and how he had worked his way up from a mere office messenger in his own country to the position he was occupying. He mentioned the enemies he had had to fight against in his ministry back home who were seeking his downfall because everyone envied his position and the perks that went with it - the honour and the glory, the money and the power.

Speaking specifically about his job as governor - to demonstrate to me the power of power - he said as the king's representative in our country, he could do anything he wanted to do in Mandzah and nothing would happen to him. Which was true, and which is equally true today, although we no longer have governors. White people continue to be more powerful in Mandzah today than our own leaders. At any rate, he said the police, military, chiefs, senior divisional officers, customs officials, and all the provinces were under his boots, and that he had been instrumental in encouraging our colonial administrators to turn our country into a cash rather than a food-crop growing country because their industries back home needed our raw materials and minerals badly for their own development.

As I write these lines now, I sense that if the AIDS virus had broken out then, we would have been forced, even by force of arms, to grow nothing else but rubber throughout the country so their factories would manufacture condoms cheaply.

When I insisted that I did not think I was particularly qualified for such a noble position of party leader, the governor laughed himself hoarse self-deprecatingly. He reeled off the names of all the key white colonial administrators in our country at the time and explained that apart from about five of them, all the others ruling the country were not really qualified; yet the country was not doing badly.

He added that the situation was not different in his own country and that once I became the leader of the party - and hopefully the leader of my country - I would realize that leading a people is not very difficult because people like being led by the nose. He explained that few people are born to rule and that I would learn the ropes on the job, especially how to manipulate people and events.

The governor then took me to a sumptuous office next to his grandiose bedroom and showed me the finest local artifacts that the various white divisional officers in the country had sent to him so that he could ship them to the museums back home in his country. I immediately understood that our history was being transferred abroad. I now understand how come one finds more original Mandzah art in white man country today than in Mandzah itself.

After seeing and hearing all these things, I started to marvel at the power of power.

To whet my appetite further, the governor took me to another room and showed me all the things that he had imported form his own country to be distributed to all his political friends in Mandzah. There were so many beautiful things there that I cannot begin to enumerate them. He assured me that I could have access to all such things if I became the leader of my country because all I had to do was snap my finger like they were doing and everything would be given to me. The sheer splendour of what I saw tantalized my fancy.

Right there in front of the governor, I started dreaming about the presidency and about being in a mansion bigger and better than his own with the whole country at my beck and call. I began to imagine myself chatting and keeping company with the kings and queens of this world, or what is left of royalty, and owning as many cars, airplanes, yachts, and castles as I was sure I would need. Without realizing it, my mind started sifting through the world's leaders, brushing aside many heads of state that I didn't believe met the high standards I had set for leaders. There's nothing as real as fantasy, and its reality can be very thrilling. I decided there and then that it would be disrespectful and discourteous of me to keep the governor guessing and not respond favourably to his request for me to lead my people. I knew paramount chiefs who ruled over dynasties and who had done everything possible to meet the governor and had been rebuffed. Here I was in the company of the highest authority in the land discussing the future of my country and the genuine prospects for me to be president. I decided immediately that I wasn't going to miss such a golden opportunity of rendering my people the utmost service it deserved.

I told the governor that I would run for the leadership of the MPU, and that I was relying on his support as they had promised. He said I shouldn't say I was going to run for the leadership because I wouldn't have to run. I was going to be made the leader of the MAPU. Just like that. There would be no elections but I would be elected. And even if there were elections, I would most definitely win or be made to win. Of course, I couldn't believe my ears. I had always thought that Africa alone had a controlling interest in gerrymandering an election.

I hope the world understands that I am emphasizing these points because most people are not fully aware of the pressures to which I was subjected to accept the leadership of my people. And since these are things that happened a very long time ago, even before independence, many people, especially the young ones, do not fully grasp what happened at that time.

Disgruntled members of the MIP and their supporters have been waging a relentless campaign against me, but I have continued to survive because my heart is clean. People say politics is a dirty game. I say politics in not dirty; people are dirty. Proof is that I have been in this business now for over fifty years and have neither soiled my hands nor dirtied my name.

4

Party Leadership

As soon as the MIP got wind of the fact that my own party, the MAPU, was planning a nationwide rally to elect me as its standard bearer, they launched a civil disobedience campaign. Since they were really more popular than my own party, those of us who were planning our rally did so with great trepidation. The MIP leader, Kwa Karangwa, was a suave speaker, a graduate form Habdard University who had returned form the United Conquerors Republic with drive and dynamism that put fear into all of us.

The MIP leader began preaching such things as independence, democratic elections, freedom of speech, free enterprise, and so on and so forth. Those things that could not put food in the bellies of our people, although they were things our young people wanted to hear. That made the MIP very popular. But the white establishment got particularly scared about the independence theme because if independence came to pass, it would mean a loss of their privileged status, their source of cheap raw materials, and the dumping ground for their products. They were especially scared that the independence virus might spread to other countries in Africa and thus result in the loss of their empire.

We, in the MAPU, were wary of people who, after spending years abroad, returned home claiming to have answers to all our problems. That is why we preached moderation, tolerance, and cohabitation. We believed justifiably that we knew the country better since all of us had followed what was happening at close range. The MIP boys had been living in the comfortable armchairs of academia abroad and had brought back foreign ideologies to impose on our people. Our argument, born out of experience, was that these people were much too young to lead the country and that they had never really held any significant office. Although they were educated, they were very careless and immature. We did not think that a country as prosperous as ours should be allowed to go to the dogs.

Some authors have wondered why we did not give room to the people to decide for themselves through fair and democratic elections. These are stupid authors because they don't know that elections in Africa, by their very nature, are neither fair nor democratic. Moreover, the question is whether the people could really decide for themselves when we know that at that time, over 90% of our people were illiterate and did not understand the foreign ideology that these fellows were ramming down their throats.

We of the MAPU refused to be caught in this dragnet of foreign-imposed ideology. We decided to collaborate with the local administration which did not take kindly to Karangwa and his filthy gang of traitors.

We were aware that the eyes of the Tubab world were focused on us and that they were watching to see how we would treat Karangwa and the MIP. We also had to be careful that while we got advice and guidance from the local white establishment, we should not let this be transparent. It would have caused a great uproar in Tubab because, while they were giving open support to Karangwa and his misguided group in support of democracy and so on, they were also supporting us because they were afraid that if the MIP assumed power, they would lose their place.

The governor advised us to tread gently. Plans were worked out to kill Karangwa in a fake car accident, but these were discarded because Karangwa, either out of premonition or betrayal by one of our men, started traveling with security guards. Besides, the MIP let it be known that it was aware that some sinister individuals were planning the assassination of its leader. We abandoned the plans.

Rev. Albert Grimm, a member of the white establishment whose religious order was one of those which came to Africa to pave the way for the arrival of white businessman, suggested that we set a thief to catch a thief. He said since Karangwa was well known to be a womanizer, we should frame him by setting him up with one of the country's most notorious prostitutes and then surprise both of them in an uncompromising position. If that did not discredit Karangwa, he said, nothing else would. Most of my colleagues bought the idea and we started working out how this could best be done by enacting different scenarios.

I have to say that I did not approve of this plan but then the people's wish is God's command. My own opinion was that a worm like Karangwa should be poisoned and done away with but my colleagues vetoed me. I honestly don't understand why they vetoed me because every body knows that cases of poisoning political foes are very rampant throughout the world. We recall only too well the poisoning of Manjong Tanjong, one of Africa's most well known revolutionaries, by his white girlfriend years ago. She had been hired by some white businessmen and landowners who panicked when they heard that if Manjong Tanjong took over the government, he would nationalize everything. If an African nationalist wants to put his head on the chopping block of civilized countries, he should talk about nationalization.

As we were putting finishing touches to Rev. Grimm's grim plan, there was a bombshell. The MIP published an article accusing the church, especially Rev. Grimm, of not doing what it preached. The vitriolic attack accused Rev. Grimm of using his position to intimidate female members of the church to succumb to his bestial instincts. Thank God, Rev. Grimm was not linked to the MAPU.

The papers were not aware that Rev. Grimm was working for us, and we knew that the MIP was in the dark as far as our links with the white establishment were concerned.

We decided that prudence would be the touchstone of our action and suspended further action until after our convention. We did not want to do anything that would jeopardize the smooth running of our convention because it was going to be a test of how well organized we were and how prepared we were to lead the country. Since the MIP considered us a bunch of illiterates, which was not entirely false, they were watching to see how our convention would go. We knew this and made sure that we prepared for it well, paying attention to every little detail.

Prior to the leadership convention, the officials of the MAPU met in the home of Mr. Steve Roberts, the chief of National Security and adviser to the governor on security matters. There were three candidates: Chief Kwifon Mbaya who had caused a stir when he had converted to Christianity the year before, Mr. Sabga Nyos, a former local bicycle repairman, and Mr. Mezah Wezah, an unassuming teacher in the Native Authority School in Ebon.

An attempt was made to choose one candidate to show that we had a united front but each candidate stood his ground. In the thinking of most of the officials of our party, Mr. Mezah Wezah was the most suitable candidate because he at least could read and write. We wanted someone who would be able to meet the challenge posed by the so-called intellectuals of the MIP.

Mr. Steve Roberts advised that he did not think education was an important criterion for leadership of our party. He cited the case of his own country where the president had never been a big intellectual. He said before their president joined politics, he had been a messenger but had turned out to be one of the best presidents in his country's history. As far as Mr. Roberts was concerned, it was probably because their own president back home had never been to school that he was one of the best presidents in history.

What Mr. Roberts said was most comforting to us because we had always thought that one had to be a great intellectual to preside over the destiny of a people. We realized that we were wrong because if one looks at the world around us, one sees that countries whose destinies are in the hands of intellectuals aren't necessarily doing better.

My own feeling was that even though we did not have to be great intellectuals, Mr. Wezeh should be chosen because he would be able to talk in the white man's language. I got to know much later that Mr. Roberts opposed Mr. Wezeh's candidacy because most of the teachers in the Native Authority School (N.A. School) were considered dyed-in-the-wool MIP supporters. Mr. Roberts was not sure of Mr. Wezeh's allegiance even though we knew that Mr. Wezeh was a staunch supporter of our party. In fact, he was one of its greatest ideologues.

Such was the climate that prevailed at that meeting. It soon turned out that all three candidates were divided along tribal lines. Chief Kwifon Mbaya, as the traditional ruler of the Mbaglum people, held sway over the largest ethnic group in the country.

Since his father, his Royal Highness, the late Chief Ndzang Menang, had refused to be converted to Christianity and had opposed the colonial administration, he had been hanged in public. Mr. Roberts was afraid that His Royal Highness, Chief Kwifon Mbaya, if elected, would exact vengeance.

On the other hand, Mr. Roberts supported Mr. Sabga Nyos, the former bicycle repairman. Most of those present opposed Mr. Nyos because of his ethnic origin. He was what was called in those days *ebooh*, that is, a slave. It was said that Mr. Nyos' ancestors had been a band of marauding tribesmen who had invaded the country and had been defeated and captured as slaves. It was therefore not fitting that such a man should lead the party. Mr. Nyos was a Wulili. Even though they were considered as slaves, and maybe because they were in fact the descendants of slaves, they were a very hard-working group. Their region was the country's breadbasket and they produced most of the so-called intellectuals at the time.

The leader of the MIP, Mr. Jiga Karangwa, was himself a Wulili. Some people felt that if Nyos was our own party leader, the Wulili would be split since thy would have to choose between two of their own, but some sober-minded people like me thought that it was very dangerous concentrating power in the hands of an already powerful economic and intellectual group. Worse, the Wulili formed the bulk of the Mandzah contingent that had fought in Europe to liberate the world from the clutches of Nazism. Mr. Roberts felt that the Wulilis were already powerful, enterprising, mean, wicked and ambitious and that if they were allowed to lead the MAPU, they might eventually overrun the entire country. All of us agreed with that analysis.

There was therefore a deadlock as to who would be chosen as the MAPU's standard-bearer. When it became obvious that the more we showed disunity, the more we were playing into the hands of the MIP, Chief Kwifon Mbaya suggested that since it seemed that none of the three candidates had party-wide acceptance, a candidate from a minority ethnic group should be chosen. There was a sigh of relief as the other candidates supported the idea.

Mr. Mezah Wezah looked in my direction and smiled. I smiled back congenially. Then he stood up and proposed to the assembled party officials that in order to ensure the success of the MAPU at the next elections, he would support my candidacy for the leadership of the party. That suggestion, I confess, took me by surprise.

Never had I in my wildest dreams - and I dare say I had had some wild ones - had I imagined that I would someday be proposed for the leadership of my party. With all the respect that is due our elders, I stood up, thanked the party officials, and said in substance that while I appreciated the honour done me, I did not think I had either the qualities or the qualifications for such a high office.

The white establishment people looked at me in utter astonishment. They were surprised that I was refusing to accept the powerful and influential task of leading my people. Mr. Roberts immediately took the floor and rang our what he thought were my strong points.

First and foremost, Mr. Roberts said I came form a relatively calm minority group that had not sided openly with any of the anti-colonial factions. Second, I had a smattering of English and would therefore be able to converse with the white establishment since there wasn't anything technical to discuss with them anyway. Third, I was literate because I had completed secondary school, especially from a mission school. Fourth, I had lived with missionaries and thus had a high sense of morality that he was sure I would bring to my public life.

For most people, there was no stench of scandal trailing me. No one had ever heard that I embezzled funds, slept with someone's wife, or killed anybody. That was a very long time ago, but today, there are roaming bands of opposition people lying to the world that what I wasn't guilty of over 30 years ago, I am guilty of today. And the world, in its typical fashion of believing lies and discarding the truth, believes them.

I just could not believe that I was being proposed as a candidate for the eventual leadership of my country. Again I pretended that I did not want the job. I should remind the reader that some months before, the governor had convinced me to seek first the political kingdom and every other thing would be added to me. After every official, including the three candidates, had taken the floor in support of my candidacy, and pleaded with me to lead the party to greener pastures, I accepted the challenge of leading my people.

It is important that I reveal these behind-the curtains business because most people are not well informed about the facts. Our next task was planning our strategy: planning how I would be presented as the compromise candidate.

Many suggestions were made but the one that made most sense and that was accepted by everyone was that made by Rev. Grimm. He suggested that in order to avoid the risk of not getting the full endorsement of the MAPU, we should concoct a plan implicating the MIP in an attempt to infiltrate our convention to blow up the place. That way there would be no convention and I would simply be declared the MAPU leader. This was an ingenious plan, and the majority of those present enthusiastically supported it.

Some people had misgivings about how it would work in practice, but the ever so resourceful Rev. Grimm pointed to his won country where these things happen everyday even though they proclaim on rooftops that they are democratic.

Rev. Grimm revealed to us that at a ruling party convention held in his country when I must still have been pulling on my mother's breasts, the opposition bribed the mistress of the ruling party candidate to leave the candidate's love letters on her table, and then faint during the convention. That way she would be transported to the hospital and the hospital staff would run to her home to take some of her personal effects and then see the letters. It worked, and the ruling party was trounced in the general elections that followed.

Rev. Grimm further disclosed what happened during another ruling party convention when, while the world watched helplessly in awe as Hitler seized country upon country, the opposition got together, framed the ruling party candidate, and won the election. He said that was the way strong nations ran their internal politics and that we should not try to be holier than the pope. After all, he pointed out, they were themselves not the originators of democracy, but rather the Greeks. Hence democracy is adaptable. His country had adapted it to suit its own way of life, just as the modern Greeks too had adapted it to suit theirs.

Another thing he mentioned was the role money plays in an election in his country. He said while technically speaking, anyone could be president in his country, it was well known that the position was reserved only for the rich and famous. One needed money to run a campaign, crisscross the country several times, pay for advertisements, entertain the press so as to benefit form rave reviews, etc.

After such persuasive arguments from a man as resourceful and revered as Rev. Grimm who knew theology, history and political science well, we all agreed that we would not only do as our colonial masters were doing in their own countries, but even innovate, breathing freshness into the stale concept of democracy.

Mr. Roberts said we needn't worry needlessly. We should ensure that the opposition MIP did not have access to bank loans and deprive them of all sources of revenue while building our own war chest. In this regard, he assured us that the Governor and the entire white establishment in Mandzah would make funds available to us to ensure our victory in the election.

He even suggested that, if need be, the governor would contact his brethren in other African countries to contribute money to our campaign fund. He, without saying openly, made it known that the whites in the other African countries were watching what was happening in Mandzah because they did not want a general stirring of the people in these countries for this would spell the end of all colonial administrations.

We thanked Mr. Roberts for the assurances he had given us and promised that we would abide by his wise and learned counsel. The onus was now on me as the proposed leader of the MAPU to do everything possible to ensure first my election and then victory for the party.

There is no need to go into too many details here but let me simply say that working out a plan to discredit the MIP was not easy because they too were watching us closely and also planning a campaign to smear the MAPU. But as fate would have it, or as God had willed it, to use Rev. Grimm's expression, internal bickering among the MIP intellectuals led to the assassination of their leader, Mr. Karangwa

We in the MAPU were overjoyed. In fact, we celebrated the glad tidings although we did not want people to know this because we would have been accused of gloating over the death of Karangwa.

An investigation was open into the assassination but the governor covered it up. To this day there is no evidence of who killed Karangwa. An over-zealous police commissioner who decided that he would unearth the entire affair was found dead in his office. Then the family of the assassinated leader thought it could take the case up in the glare of the international press' searching lights. We sent emissaries to plead with them to drop the case but they were defiant. Mrs. Nyango Karangwa and her entire brood of children were involved in a ghastly road accident that claimed all their lives.

We had arranged with one of their family friends to go to their home early one morning to report that Karangwa's mother was very ill, and that she wanted Mrs. Karangwa to bring her grandchildren to see her immediately since she suspected she would die. At the same time, we had also arranged with a timber truck driver to overrun the Karangwas.

To ensure that we were above suspicion as a party, we were the first to condemn the deaths. We called for a commission of enquiry and recommended that the colonial administration should set up a trust fund to take care of what was left of the family: Karangwa's ailing mother who died form chagrin five months later, and his two children attending university in Tubab. An investigation was launched but the director of the Traffic Police department was summoned to report that Mrs. Karangwa had been driving under the influence of alcohol and had not respected traffic regulations

5

Party Convention and my Investiture

The death of Mr. Karangwa, leader of the MIP, was the most shocking news that hit the whole country. The only other event that had ever mobilized the entire country was the death of 56 workers of the railway corporation. The nation had been stunned that the colonial administration had not only failed to provide good working conditions for the railway workers but had refused to pay the families of the dead men any benefits.

It was widely assumed that members of our party had murdered Karangwa in cold blood, but that was certainly false. To dispel these baseless rumours, the MAPU convinced the governor and the white establishment to give Karangwa a fitting burial and to take care of his family.

Following Karangwa's death, the MIP was in disarray. The MAPU convention was just around the corner and the MIP needed to elect a new leader before the elections that were going to take place in about four months.

Somehow, the death of Karangwa stirred the imagination of our own party and drew attention to the fickleness of life. The MAPU vowed to stand by me as its only leader to ensure victory at the polls.

The convention was just a formality since all the spadework had been done. Our party had informed the heads of all the MAPU delegations to announce to the country and the world that they were backing me because I was the only one that could unite the party. Since I was literate, by the standards of that period, and came form a minority tribe, it was said I alone could heal the nation's wounds. The MIP distributed tracts on the eve of our party convention depicting me as a bloodthirsty, irreverent political neophyte who, if elected, would stand in the way of our people's onward march to independence. I was accused of collaborating with the colonial administration and of disrespecting our traditional rulers.

On the day of the convention, the other MAPU members that had initially been proposed as candidates for the leadership of the party took the floor and announced that they were not candidates and that they were backing my candidacy. The convention broke into spirited applause and I was elected by acclamation as the leader of the MAPU.

A few months after my election as standard-bearer of my party, I organized national elections that thrust me in the national and international limelight. After winning a landslide victory hands down with 99.99% of the votes, the governor, missionaries, and the entire white establishment were elated that their candidate had won, and they trumpeted the news abroad. The MAPU received many messages from other parties and I was soon the object of great public curiosity.

I remember receiving letters, postcards, and cables from various parts of the world. Foreign news organs that, up to that point had neglected our country suddenly became fascinated with the triumph of democracy in Mandzah. It was widely published that if elections in Africa were going to be that honest and democratic, the white establishment had nothing to fear as we would be governed by the rule of law.

My first public act as leader of the MAPU was to convene a meeting of my party's caucus to thank all party stalwarts who had made my election possible. I was especially indebted to the three candidates who had abstained in my favour: Chief Kwifon Mbaya, Mr. Sabga Nyos and Mr. Mezeh Wezeh. They pledged their loyalty to me and their full allegiance to the party and promised to work together with me so that the MAPU would triumph in future elections.

The meeting took place in a serene atmosphere. We were extremely happy at the results of the election especially as the MIP was in disarray. They had planned a well-orchestrated campaign to upstage my election but my party militants had sensed it and launched an effective public relations campaign extolling the unity of the MAPU and vaunting my impeccable credentials for the leadership of the party.

6

From Pluralism to Single Party

In order to quell public disaffection with politics, my party, the MAPU, decided that the main plank of our development policy would be a single instead of a multi-party system. It was with some fear that I listened to the reasons being advanced by both advocates and opponents of the strategy.

Anyone who has taken an objective look at the pre-single-party period in my country's history will agree that it was a crises-riddled period that detracted the government and the people form the prodigious boots-strapping task of nation-building. Politicians and party potentates of all stripes, in the name of democracy, went haywire stoking political passions and whipping their supporters into a frenzy of idolatrous hero-worship. Development projects were stalled because of politicking; students abandoned classes to stump the country on behalf of politicians; corruption reached endemic proportions and the country dithered and floundered. We in the MAPU felt constrained to respond to the alarm-bells that were ringing.

We convened a caucus of party luminaries to chart a new political course for the country. It was obvious to us that the multi-party system would not work and that time had come to make new political calculations to save the country form sliding into abysmal chaos. We knew that the eyes of the world were riveted on us and that we had to tread softly especially as conditions were ripe for a revolt. While developed countries had taken centuries to build the foundation of their democratic ideals, they expected us to do it in a few years.

Our belief was that the multi-party system goes with education. The national unity, which we were striving to forge, could not succeed if we allowed ethnic rivalries, clannishness and tribalism - in the name of multi-party politics - to stand in our way. We knew that our people were not politically mature to vote for candidates on the basis of their ideology. They would vote rather along tribal lines. Until we had a sense of unity and nationhood, until our people transcended petty tribal jealousies, I was not going to be an advocate of multi-party politics because it would have torn apart the fabric of our fragile unity.

Having said this, my government believed that while so-called democracy was not a panacea to our problems, we would allow the people to freely choose their representatives. Within the framework of our single national party, we were going to allow anyone who wanted to stand for an elective office to do so in his or her constituency. But this was going to be done within the framework of the MAPU. In other words, we were not against the people choosing their representatives but rather against the proliferation of political parties along tribal lines. The unity of Mandzah is sacred to us, and we did not want to auction it on the altar of political expediency to please the Western world and ingratiate ourselves with them.

In preparation for the ushering in of the single-party system, our party kingpins met privately in my home to work out a strategy before submitting whatever our proposals were to the rank and file of the party. Somehow, as it usually happens, someone from the opposition got wind of our plans and started to talk. We sent Mr. Lloyd Keith Benson, one of our white supporters, to send out signals to the fellow that if he did not sew his mouth, we would chew his tongue.

To establish a single-party rule, one must be very careful and proceed with extreme caution. The so-called developed world is always quick to stigmatize single-party regimes, and sometimes poses the adoption of multi-party politics as a condition for further assistance. Besides, with the mounting opposition we had from our students abroad and from disenchanted political lackeys, we knew that we had to move as if we were in a minefield.

Our party strategists met several times to determine the best way to proceed. We decided that for the single-party idea to gain currency and credence, it must be made to appear as if the people proposed it since the people can never go wrong.

But even if the idea won wide acclaim, we knew that even under the multi-party system, some developed countries had in the past refused to accept the verdict of the people especially when the party elected espoused views that went against their self-seeking interests. In other words, there is nothing really like democracy; one just had to make it appear that one was democratic.

We sent fire-spitting emissaries with an almost evangelical devotion to our party to scour the country and preach the doctrine of unity, peace and stability. Our strategy was simple: point out to the chiefs that they were far better under us than under some unknown profit-seeker masquerading as a political leader.

We pointed to the countless development projects we had undertaken: the cars we had promised we would buy for the chiefs, the beautiful homes my ministers built and leased at exorbitant cost to the government for its ministers, the thousands of foreign cars on our streets, the availability of all brands of imported foods and luxury goods, the numerous prestige projects strewn all over our capital city to give the world the semblance of our development (such as the tall 7-story building in the centre of our capital city built by my wife and leased to the government), the evergreen golf course that has become an attraction to our foreign friends although our people do not understand that it is not a public toilet, etc.

Another astute strategy we adopted was to play on the tribal sensibilities of the traditional rulers. We proved to them that tribalism was the cancer destroying our country. The MIP, for example, though very popular, was made up mostly of individuals from Mr. Karangwa's tribe who were well known to be very lazy. They claimed to have seen the white man first, and thus believed that they were black man white man. Yet when it came to developing the country, they just folded their arms and waited for their so-called slaves from the hinterland to do all the work.

On the other hand, people from my own ethnic group held the reins of power. Though in the minority, they held the country's purse strings and occupied most strategic positions in government and industry. I did this intentionally to counterbalance the potent political force of Karangwa's people.

The single-party idea was developed to show the people that tribalism would be eradicated and that national unity would be forged. Elements of the MIP were adverse to this proposal. They opposed us openly, published tracts, and portrayed me as some power-grabbing idiot from the political backwoods who wanted to subjugate the country to my indomitable will.

The Western press joined the fray with lecture upon lecture on the sanctity of democratic ideals that they themselves do not respect. While it is technically true that any citizen in Tubab (white man country) can be president, I have yet to see or be told of a citizen without the necessary financial backing who was ever elected president. In most cases, the wrong people are usually elected because they have the financial resources and logistics to make a lot of noise and promises everyone knows in advance they can't keep.

It is surprising how, straining under the weight of the problem we were facing, I remained lucid and did not allow the ranting of a few misguided individuals to subvert a natural process of political evolution. We continued to lay the basis for our people to spontaneously propose the idea of a single party.

In order to neutralize the majority tribe, which in fact had no political, economic or military backing, we decided to co-opt some of their leading lights into our party. The minister of information, disinformation, propaganda and censorship, Mr. Talktrue Nodelie, contacted one Mr. Ntad Keju, minister without portfolio in the MIP shadow cabinet because he was most vulnerable to blackmail. We threatened to blackmail Mr. Ntad Keju for going out with one Tubab missionary woman if he did not cross the carpet to our party. We coached Keju to announce that after much soul-searching, he was crossing the carpet to join the MAPU because he felt our party was the only one that could deliver our people from the shackles of poverty, illiteracy, disunity and looming civil strife. We promised him a cabinet position if he acted his part well.

Ntad Keju performed beyond our own wildest expectations. He made it appear that he had requested the minister of information, disinformation, propaganda and censorship to allow him address a press conference on an important allegation that had been made by members of his own party. Normally, we never allowed the opposition to use the country's mass media, but we agreed, exceptionally, to allow Ntad Keju to go on the airwaves.

Keju dressed in his finest traditional robes befitting a man of his stature since he was the successor to his late father's estate. He started rightly by paying deserved tribute to me, His Excellency Wan Nei, Chairman of the MAPU, Commander-in-Chief of the Mandzah Armed Forces, Keeper of the National Till, Chairman of the National Council of Traditional Rulers, Father of the Nation, Chancellor of the Mandzah National University, Depository of National Wisdom, Father of Orphans, Husband of Widows, and Supreme Leader of Mandzah.

Keju said he had asked to meet the press to quash the invidious rumours that were being circulated by some mischievous minds to the effect that he was dilly-dallying with Mrs. Comfort Stone, wife of a Tubab missionary. Mr. Keju swore that while he knew the Stones, he had never been privileged to see the colour of Mrs. Stone's bra and panty.

He then added, much to the delight of the press, that since he was not a televangelist, he did not know how to go about wooing a missionary's wife and that, as a bachelor, he had access to any single woman he wanted and thus did not see why he would mess round with a married woman.

"Why should I, a bachelor," Ntad Keju asked, "love one miserable, lonely bird when a chorus, with all its binding melody, tastes sweeter than the twang of a single runaway bird?"

That question became an instant hit and musicians gave it a melody. The records and cassettes sold like hot cakes.

Keju went further to say that he knew that pleasure, when illicit, pleases pleasurably but that he had never given thought to an illicit affair especially as he did not want to blame himself in death for having refused to hearken to the call of his conscience.

Keju then said he had given serious thought to the way the country was evolving and realized that too many parties spoil the presidential broth. He had therefore decided to put his country first and that there could not be a better way of doing this than crossing the carpet to the MAPU which was the people's party.

That news was a bomb and given the press' penchant for over-dramatization of events, the nation was stunned.

Keju's performance had been superb and he instantly became a household name; he who, until then, had been relegated by society to the backwoods of politics.

The MIP was understandably shocked and outraged. We prodded the media to sing the news everyday, and it sang it melodiously to the rhythm of editorials, feature articles, talk shows and so on. Slowly the people began to suspect that something must be terribly wrong with the MIP and that, decapitated of a leader as it had been following Karangwa's death, it was a ship without a captain.

We chimed in and showed the country and the world that the MIP was ungovernable and that as such it could not be expected to govern a country, which was made up of several warrior tribes.

We planned yet another major coup. We encouraged three MIP party stalwarts to vie for the leadership of their party and promised each of them assistance. The three, Kom Ngumba, Abel Tumnyam and Chronicles Wumu announced to the nation that they would contest the leadership of the MIP. Again that news was a bombshell. Being form different ethnic regions, and representing various interest groups, the MIP was soon split not only along tribal lines but also along social and political lines.

Ngumba was from a small village in the forest region, Nap, and he was the favourite of the traditional rulers who saw him as a defender of the role of traditional rulers in a modern context. Abel Tumnyam was from the coastal region like my minister of energy, mines and power.

The coastal people always claimed to have seen the white man first and thrived on the fantasy of vainglory. But most politicians liked the coastal people because they were usually neutral. Their main interest was music and the good life. Besides, they were so few that they did not constitute a force to reckon with.

Chronicles Wumu was the son of one of the first well-known Mandzah pastors who had been grooming his son to serve God. Chronicles said he did not see why he could not serve God and politics. His argument was that he would be a more effective servant of God if he was a good servant of the people.

The stage was thus set for a grueling electoral round robin match pitting each of these three candidates against the other. We sat back and watched the MIP tear itself to pieces.

7

Appointments in Government

Of all the thankless tasks that a president performs, none is as demanding of his time, wits and intelligence as the appointment of cabinet ministers. This is one domestic chore I would rather do without, but then it also happens to be one of the most important functions of a president.

Many people do not know that before I undertake any major cabinet reshuffle, I have to spend days agonizing over who to appoint to what position and for how long. I sometimes even consult my witch doctor. I have to be sure that the minister is wedded to my philosophy and that he will perform my will. That is not easy in a country like mine in which there are so many ethnic groups that I must seek to appease.

Then, of course, there is the issue of qualifications for the job. Too many people have made political mileage out of this but as far as I am concerned, anybody can be a minister since thy get their direction and guidelines directly from me. I initiate all policies and all thee ministers have to do is implement them. Where they have to use their discretion, they must ensure that it is within the guidelines laid down by the party.

I have decided, on the basis of my own experience and that of my colleagues in other countries, that being an intellectual is not necessarily a passport for employment. I don't think there are intellectuals anywhere in the world as dishonest as those we have in Africa. They will criticize anything government does but when they are put in positions where they are supposed to influence government policy, they acquiesce and start politicking because they want better positions.

I shall discuss some of the criteria that potential ministers must meet. But before I do so, I believe it would be useful to discuss what has come to be known as my inner circle.

Inner circle

I know of no president worthy of the name who does not have an inner circle, a closely-knit unit of family, friends, hangers on, etc. These are the people whom the President listens to first. The rest he plays by the ear.

Because the inner circle helps formulate policy, manipulates the president, and is only interested in wielding its own power over the president, there is usually a lot of infighting. A good president is usually one who knows precisely how to manipulate the inner circle and to pit each member against the other. But this depends very much on how the president chooses his men. I shall open up my inner circle to the searching eyes of the world like no president has ever done.

Drivers

I am lucky that I have been using the same driver for over 35 years. Dotilaso Famiredo has become like a family member since I recruited him as my chief driver even before I became president. Because he is honest, servile and loyal, he is the only one I can trust.

Trust is very important in politics although most people do not realize it. Just as a president must have full trust and confidence in the people that he appoints to key positions, he must not forget the little ones who run his small errands on a daily basis.

It is true that all presidents, especially African presidents, are gods in some way, but they are also very human. It is therefore understandable that our people should give us titles out of the great love they have for us. Some of us have been compared to the strongest and fiercest animals in the world while others have been called The Guide, The Father of the Nation, The Father of Independence, The Divine Messenger, The Supreme Leader, etc. Honour to whom honour is due. Those of us who are leaders appreciate the outpouring of love that our people have been manifesting to us. I call my driver by his title-driver.

For someone like me who is the Father of the Nation, I must ensure that everyone looks up to me as an incarnation of patriotism, hard work, discipline, and honesty. A driver can be very useful in helping a president to project this image.

My driver, Mr. Famiredo, knows me so well that he knows exactly what I want and when I want it. For example, he knows exactly the kind of women I like to fool around with and how to keep tabs on the drivers of my ministers so as to report to me what they are saying about their bosses.

Given the confidence I have in Famiredo, I usually first discuss any decision I intend to take with him in order to find out what the reaction of the common man will be. I must say that Famiredo shows great insight in the analysis of political and especially economic issues although, as an expert driver, he would much rather debate scientific and cultural issues.

Unlike most members of my inner circle, however, Famiredo also has a sharp wit and sixth sense. One of my trusted aides once gave him a note directing him to take a particular road where my car would be ambushed, but Famiredo was very smart and foresighted. He turned to me blithely on the way and handed me the map of the area so I could direct him since he could not read and write. This is clear proof, if ever there was any doubt that one does not have to be literate to be smart.

Cooks and household help

I refuse, on the counsel of Dr. Moneyhard Achucho, my personal medicine man, or what is called in the esoteric language of politics, my personal physician, to reveal any information on those who cook for me and take care of my living quarters. It may, however, please the world to learn that our chief cook is expected by law to taste my food. Parliament was forced to enact this law after the former speaker of our National Assembly collapsed and died after tasting my food.

With regard to the other household staff (cleaners, gardeners, butlers, guards, elevator attendants, baby sitters, carpet cleaners and carpet crossers, etc.), suffice it to say that they have been discharging their duties and responsibilities with patriotism and love for me.

A story appeared in the *Kongosa* magazine purporting to be an interview with my fourth wife, Her Majesty, Watoh Lendut. She is reported to have said that she loves to cook and carry out other domestic chores. That is not true. Since I became president, I

stopped eating magabtari, the only dish she knows how to cook.
Secretaries

As anyone who is important enough to have a secretary knows, a good secretary is a boss' closest aide and confidante. I know some bosses who consider that their secretaries are more important than their spouse and sometime allow their secretary to double as their spouse. I can't say I haven't gone that far.

For those who know Mandzah well, they will agree with me that there are many bosses in this country who run away from home because of their secretary. People believe, erroneously, of course, that we presidents don't know what is happening in our country. A few years ago, there was a mighty scandal because the director of repression in the ministry of the armed forces abandoned his wife and 11 children and moved in with his secretary who had also abandoned her husband and 8 children. People came to entreat me to fire the director and I refused on the grounds that I'm not sure I can find a sensible director in Mandzah who hasn't a second home away from home.

My personal secretary is Mrs. Julia Green, a white woman about whom much has been written and said. People have said all sorts of things about us, but we couldn't be bothered. She remains my most trusted secretary. Accusations that she passes secrets to foreign powers are as diabolical as they are untrue. What secrets do we have that will remain secrets for long? It is precisely because I know that secrets tantalize our imagination for openness that I am running a secret government.

To squelch persistent rumours that Mrs. Green is my girlfriend, Julia and I agreed that she should marry Field Marshall Dogo Godo of our revered armed forces who had just left his wife for a young schoolgirl. The Godos now have four lovely children but slanderous minds have stooped to say that the children are mine. Let me assure my people that this President does not mess round with his people's wives.

Other Key appointments
Ministers

I mentioned earlier the importance of selecting the right people to fill key positions in government to give the impression that the government's policies are being implemented. In appointing staff, the president uses his judgment as to the suitability of the individual for the position, and takes into account other considerations such as ethnic and religious representation. In a country like ours that has myriads of ethnic groups and is divided between Moslems and non-Moslems, the president must be very discerning in his choice of the key staff that will implement his policies.

In thirty years, I have made about 15 major cabinet reshuffles and about 5 minor ones. Major reshuffles entail the sacking of at least half the cabinet for reasons ranging from treachery, disloyalty, and embezzlement to over-popularity. Contrary to press reports, no minister has ever been sacked for incompetence. All my ministers are very incompetent.

There have been some controversial appointments in the past that have rankled our donor friends. I remember that pressure was brought to bear on me not to appoint Nyamatud Wanmutah as minister of finance, pre-finance, debts and liquidation. Wanmutah, for all I know, was a great militant of our party and had been treasurer of the church in his village. Having been in charge of the fiscal policy of his church, and having successfully reined in expenditure and forced every member of the congregation to pay a certain amount monthly as church offering, I was convinced that he had the right qualifications for the job. We needed someone with his experience in extorting money in that position.

Our donor friends, because of a fistful of dollars they were going to give us, insisted that I should not appoint Wanmutah because they claimed he did not have international experience, and that he would not be able to implement the tough measures they had laid down as a condition for giving us the money. My government resisted the measures because they were going to lead to more suffering for our people who were already crumbling under the yoke of economic crisis. Our donor friends wouldn't listen to our explanations and got together to boycott my government so as to incite the people to riot.

After a year of blackmail by the donor community, which cut off all food and military aid, I saw the folly of my ways and demoted Wanmutah to some junior minister position.

Ambassadors

An ambassador is a president's representative in a foreign country and must, accordingly, be someone in whom the president has absolute trust and confidence to represent the country and explain government policy.

Because of the high premium that my country places on its security and also on bilateral relations, my government has endeavoured, notwithstanding the high cost, to maintain fully staffed embassies in nearly every country on the face of the earth. Of course, this costs us a lot of money especially as most of our diplomats have a horde of children and family members that they take with them abroad at government's expense. Government has to pay their passage, medical bills, rents, etc. last year some of our embassy staff were kicked out of their homes because we hadn't paid their rents in over two years. In some cases, the rents were sent but the diplomats diverted the money to other uses. As much as we recognize that this situation does our country dishonour, it is preposterous for people to suggest that I dip into our personal national account to meet these expenses. Why should I use my personal fortune to pay for government expenses? Which president does this anywhere in the world? I think civilized society should use the same yardstick to measure all presidents.

In any case, notwithstanding the high cost of maintaining so many embassies, we believe all of them are necessary. We need embassies all over the world to explain our policies to our foreign partners and to spy on our nationals. Accordingly, our embassy staff is drilled in the art of gathering information on our students, businessmen visiting foreign countries, and government delegations. We believe that, as a young country still groping its way in the vortex of international affairs, we should not appoint inexperienced individuals to such sensitive diplomatic posts.

The staff of our embassies are chosen from the ministry of foreign matters, the department of state security, the gendarmerie, and customs. However, more often than not, I appoint them myself depending on their allegiance to the government and me. We need people who know government policy well and who can speak eloquently on my behalf in any forum abroad. I was forced last year to recall Ambassador Kwali Likwa from the United

Nations because he couldn't read his own speech. I had appointed him to that position in recognition of his past services to our party and not in view of his ridiculing the party and his country in front of the world.

There are two classes of ambassadors in my country: career civil servants and political appointees. I have adopted the policy of selecting my ambassadors along tribal lines and on the basis of their popularity. For example, the majority of my country's ambassadors are from my own ethnic group because they understand my language and can readily defend government policy. Then, as in the case of Lieutenant Atara Angenge who was so popular that everyone was saying that if he made a coup it would be successful, I simply banished him to far away Mben where he is vegetating in our embassy.

My minister of foreign matters has, after a careful investigation confirmed the rumour that appeared in one of our national dailies, the *Oracle*. It would appear that some of my ambassadors have used their positions to enrich themselves. They sell passports, divert state funds to their own use, present bogus or padded receipts, and so on. My own investigations show that this is indeed the case. But then ambassadors are answerable to me and only to me and the minister of foreign matters had no business recommending that I recall some of these ambassadors.

We all know that the success of any security operation depends on the secrecy with which it is cloaked. I have instructed my ambassadors to use state funds carefully and to make sure that there is absolutely no evidence of what the funds are used for. The last thing we want is for some nosy journalist or opposition gangster to lay their hands on documents dealing with our security slush funds, especially with respect to our joint activities with the Tubab security services.

8

Policies in Some Key Sectors

At a time when our raw materials are no longer fetching us mush foreign exchange, my government has decided to revamp the various sectors of the economy by taking some very painful and drastic decisions. We are not unmindful of the sacrifices made by our people in these had times, but we appeal to them to bear with us and cooperate with the government in its struggle to relieve the nation of the harsh effects of the economic crisis.

Economic planning

It must be admitted that Mr. Achiri Munoh Nyanga, my minister of economic planning and development plans, who the Tubabs would have preferred that I second to the International Lenders Association, it must be admitted, was ahead of his time. He had the foresight years ago to introduce our own currency so we could mint our own money at will instead of tying our Kapa to the apron strings of some foreign currency. We had been subjugated for too long to the harsh monetary policies of the Tubab government because we were using their money. By introducing the Mandzah Kapa, we were able to control our currency and to print any amount we needed at any time. As a result, a lot of money is floating in the country.

Our economists are divided over the merits and demerits of having our own currency. We think the argument is purely academic because we have benefited more from having our own currency than if we did not have it. The government, for example, has refused to go broke or to declare bankruptcy.

People point to the shortage of foreign exchange and our thriving black market and lay the blame at the door of our local currency. We in the government see the problem differently. We do not see anything wrong with having our own currency because we are then able to use the little foreign exchange that exists carefully, distributing it to key sectors of the economy through political friends.

For those who have some knowledge of economics, it is to be expected that because we have our own currency, foreign currency may be hard to come by especially as our cash crops can no longer fetch us much hard currency. These are the hard facts of life and I have appealed to my people to live with them.

The little hard currency that we manage to earn from the few tourists that visit our country and from the mortgage we earn on the country in the form of underdevelopment aid and assistance is used very sparingly. This government is very concerned about our country's future. Accordingly, when a little foreign currency trickles into the country, it is immediately repatriated for safe keeping in our personal national bank account abroad. From time to time some of it is used to undertake priority development programs. For example, to pay for the President's official and private trips, to purchase castles and homes abroad, to bribe foreign journalists, foreign politicians and lobbyists, opposition leaders, the church, etc. The relative stability of my government and the peace we enjoy in Mandzah is proof that the development objectives we set for ourselves when we achieved independence are being achieved.

Another wise decision that Nyanga took was to raise taxes. We are not like the Tubabs for whom taxes are an economic and political scarecrow or albatross. Our people understand that in order for government to provide all the services that the people need, there must be money in government's coffers. Money, unhappily for most of us, does not grow on trees.

Where on this African continent do people live as luxuriously as those of us in Mandzah? All our ministers drive around in the best imported luxury cars, and we provide them with generous salaries and fringe benefits – free house, electricity, water, unlimited telephone calls anywhere in the world, car for madam, car for the children, car for shopping. All former members of parliament too have generous salaries for life as a sign of gratitude to them for their contribution to the underdevelopment of this country and for their accepting to be disbanded so I can rule without reporting to anybody. They still maintain their parliamentary privileges and immunities and live in furnished government quarters.

Our ambassadors abroad, being my personal representatives, have been authorized to spend as much as they want to ensure that our security as a people is maintained. We believe, unlike most other people, that the fruits of our labour must be shared equitably and that the national cake is big enough to go round.

Our policy is guided by our concern to ensure that all officials of government live well so that the rest of the population will try to rise to their level. This explains why Nyanga took the bold and courageous step of imposing heavy taxes on the majority of the population. It made great sense because taxing the majority of the population was going to bring in more tax money than taxing a few rich government officials who get everything free anyway.

Another sound economic measure Nyanga took was the fine-tuning of the very successful unemployment policy that we adopted thirty years ago and that many African and Third World countries have stolen from us. The policy is based on the premise that since we rely on the developed and civilized world for everything we need, we should pawn our country to them for some time. When they are sick and tired of running it, they will return it to us. Our reasoning is that they love us like a child loves his toy, but a child soon gets fed up playing with the same toy all the time.

We have had to be making cosmetic and serious adjustments to the unemployment policy to adapt it to current realities. As the number of graduates increases, so too should unemployment. We are gratified that this is one area in which we have done exceeding well, and we should like to express sincere thanks to the International Loan Shark Fund which has all along been most helpful in counseling us and giving guidance in the way the policy should be implemented for maximum results to be obtained.

When Mandzah achieved independence, little did we know then that we had the necessary human resources and potential to rein in employment and enhance unemployment. We also did not think the time was ripe to prevent our citizens from occupying positions of influence. After a trial period of 30 years, we have concluded that we were wrong, and we have mustered the courage to say so. Our people have been very indulgent and have reaffirmed their confidence and faith in us by re-electing me several times to enable me continue the good work I began over 30 years ago.

Confidence must be merited, and everyone will agree with me that I am responding in kind to my people's trust in me and my team.

Since last year we have decided that it makes both economic and political sense to bring in as many Tubab nationals (we call them experts) as possible to occupy key positions in government and in the economy. We will continue to open our borders to our brothers and sisters from other African countries but they will not be considered as experts. Tubabs and Tubabs alone have the right to be called experts.

An expert, as far as my government is concerned, is a Tubab who, for lack of gainful employment in his or her country, decides to forego all the benefits accruing to him or her by virtue of their country being very developed and civilized (crime, drugs, incest, solitude, junk mail, insecurity, loans, murder, etc.) to take up a key technical or advisory position in a developing country and to suffer the most ignominious deprivations (skyrocketing salary inversely proportional to qualifications and to duties performed, dirt cheap labour, lack of crime and drugs, peace of mind, absence of discrimination, etc.).

My government has weighed the advantages of hiring Tubab experts against the hiring of our nationals in Tubab and has concluded that the employment of Tubabs in Mandzah is not directly correlated with Mandzah employment in Tubab. That is a fact. The Tubabs send us their unemployable nationals and we sent them our employable ones. We gain because we cannot recruit our employable nationals and they gain because they cannot recruit their unemployable ones. This is what is called balanced trade.

As far as salaries for Tubab experts are concerned, we take a number of economic, social, political and cultural parameters into consideration. First of all, the longer the Tubab unemployed and soon-to-be Mandzah expert remained unemployed, the higher their salaries. And the lower their qualifications, the higher their salaries still. We have to make employment conditions in Mandzah as attractive to our Tubab friends as possible since we need them badly for our underdevelopment.

Since we need Tubab experts, we also have to implement those policies that will help discourage our own nationals who have finished school from taking up jobs that we have reserved for the Tubabs. In furtherance of this policy, the minister of labour, trade unions, strikes and unemployment took a number of measures aimed at encouraging our employable nationals to remain abroad, and those at home to choose unemployment abroad, also.

1. We have requested all our embassies to desist from encouraging our young employable nationals from returning home. We did not send them to school abroad so they will return home. With the high level of training they have received, they can stay in Tubab and drive taxis, clean offices, work as farm hands, and so on and so forth. However, those of them who are members of our party and who have testimonials to show that they have denounced many of their colleagues in the opposition, will be welcomed home with deserved honours and plum jobs.
2. We understand that some of our intellectuals occupy key positions in Tubab and that they are so good that the Tubabs are reluctant to let them quit. We say bravo to Tubab. We are honoured that our Tubab friends too want our technical assistance even though our nationals are being paid lover salaries than their Tubab colleagues with the same qualifications and experience.
3. We have maintained that given the distressful state of our economy, we cannot afford to recruit, let alone provide adequate working conditions and facilities to our young graduates.
4. After studying the recommendation made by the Presidential Task Force on Unemployment, we have concluded that it is not proper at this time to reduce the retirement age. There are a lot of senior citizens in government (for example, ministers, ambassadors, party kingpins, managing directors, etc.) who will become wards of the state if they retired today. While it is true that they have amassed a fortune over the years, it is also true that there is nothing as deadly to the national psyche as idleness, especially for people who have been dyed-in-the-wool party stalwarts all their life. They are old but still sprightly and we should not abandon them now. We do not want to be like the Tubabs who banish their

senior citizens to homes. We'll maintain ours in government until death do us part.

5. For those privileged enough to be working in government, the party has decided that early next year all civil servants should declare their age. The situation as we have it today is too confusing. Many civil servants have official versus their real age. How can one explain the fact that there are still in government many definitely old people but who are officially teenagers? We should respect rather than be ashamed of our age. Government is not a social club, and it is not because grandfathers and grandmothers are marrying or sleeping with partners that are younger than their children that they should think it gives them the right to work and die in government. Besides, we are not in the Holy Woods where people maintain the same age perpetually. Our civil servants cannot afford the cost of face-lifts, and should therefore match their age to their looks.

6. In order to further encourage Tubab experts to come to our country to hasten the pace of our underdevelopment, we shall, in addition to paying them generous salaries, continue to offer them generous fringe benefits, including a malaria allowance. Tubabs dread malaria and since, notwithstanding their unfathomable medical expertise, they do not seem to be able to contain the disease, maybe because it is supposed to afflict only citizens of the tropical world, we have to reward the few of them who brave it and come to work in our country. Each Tubab expert will be entitled to a free house and utilities, free car and gasoline, entertainment allowance, air tickets every three months for the family to and from Tubab, and other negotiable benefits.

With regard to the private sector we shall continue to be just as generous with our Tubab friends. We do not believe in tit for tat. Although everyone knows that the Tubabs maltreated us during the colonial times, and still do, we take the very dim view that the colonial period is over for good and that only they can help us revive our sluggish private sector since they were the ones who impeded its development from the beginning. We must have faith in our Tubab friends. They know us well. We will therefore give appropriate incentives to Tubab businessmen to compete favourably with our own businessmen. Since they have more capital than our people, they do not have to pay taxes, and as we are about to embark on our privatization scheme, we need their capital. The Privatization Committee has already drawn up a list of the public-owned corporations that we shall auction to them depending, of course, on the amount of commission paid in advance. Our indigenous businessmen are indigent. They say they cannot pay the commissions immediately and have thus been struck off the list of bidders.

Last year, a group of Mandzah businessmen and officials of the Chamber of Commerce flocked to the People's House to query me about my business reform program. This confrontation came in the wake of a meeting I had had in my office with a visiting Tubab delegation that was in our country to discuss a joint venture with government. My wife was looking for partners with money to purchase our diamonds and gold mines as well as oil wells.

When we had the single-party system, it was reasonably cheap to run an election since all our nationals, with the exception of a few stubborn ones, were forced to be members of our national party. Every citizen had to travel with their party membership card otherwise they would be arrested and detained. Before elections, every major village and organized group of individuals (trade unions, students, market women, teachers and professors, the Bar Association, churches, businessmen, etc.) would send a petition to me to run as the sole candidate because I had done so much for the country. The radio and television would read out the petitions during every newscast for weeks on end to show to the doubting world out there that I am the one in whom the people are well pleased. The results were always known in advance since I was the only candidate: 99.99%. We in Africa did not invent elections, but we know how to use them.

Over the last few years that street demonstrations have forced us to grudgingly accept the multi-party system, things have changed. Enemies of our people have been going round sowing the seed of hate in our people's mind about me. They claim that I haven't been doing anything in over 30 years as if all I have been doing is sleeping. There is no doubt that I have been sleeping, but I have never claimed to have the gift of hibernation, nor am I a fossil.

I have a clean record for everyone to see. In order to counter these claims, we have had to censor newspapers and bribe some key opposition people to cross over to our side. From our experience, most of our nationals who go into the opposition do so because thy want money and power. My government therefore looks for money wherever it can to buy over opposition people before elections. It was for this reason that we were looking for partners to buy our gold, diamonds and oil wells.

I do not know why the press likes to poke its nose in matters that do not concern it. One toilet-tissue tabloid reported that if the deal went through, I stood to make about one million dollars from it. I found that allegation to be baseless, without foundation and in poor taste. What is one million dollars to me, or for that matter to any of my African colleagues when each one of us has a personal fortune that is more than our country's gross national product? I remember that when the so-called opposition collective of political parties wanted to form a coalition to fight me in the last elections, I called some of their leaders and gave them a bagful of dollars and they immediately changed their minds and supported me. That is not all. I dish out such desultory amounts day in day out when I visit different parts of the country. I usually carry small parcels and envelopes for the chiefs, senior officers of the armed forces, etc.

I think it is insulting for our newspapers to insinuate that while most African leaders are competing with each other to amass a fortune for themselves, the president of Mandzah should lag behind. Our people should have a sense of patriotism and encourage their president to do better than the others. Certainly, we have been doing exceedingly well in all the other sectors of underdevelopment. Recently, for example, I was declared Mandzah's foremost farmer because I own the largest coffee, pineapples, sugar cane and banana plantations. To make life easier for our farmers, the ministry of agriculture decided that since its staff was spending most of its time and resources working for me on my farms, we should disband the farmers cooperatives and the marketing board so that farmers should go through me to market their produce. Unfortunately, as a result of the depressed state of the international economy, I have had to drastically reduce the producer price I have been paying to the farmers competing against me.

A responsible press must be responsible. We have stated that we stand for press freedom, but we do not wish the press to take its freedom for granted because freedom, when not won by hard struggle, is very easily abused.

Tourism

We have decided to give pride of place to our young tourist industry by constructing more hotels and motels to make it easier for tourists and visitors to our country to find comfortable accommodation. We will give every encouragement to these people by giving incentives to our girls and boys to sleep with them. They need the money, and so too does the government.

I cannot resist the temptation of using my binoculars every Sunday afternoon to peep from my study and behold the naked white women lying on our beaches flat on their backs, soaking in the radiant Mandzah sun, and airing all parts of their body.

It is obvious that these tourists and visitors do not come to our country for lack of other places to go to. There is indeed keen competition in the tourist industry and if we hope to win as many of these people as possible, then we must be creative and innovative.

I challenge every citizen who loves his country to rise up to this national challenge and suggest ways and means of boosting the tourist trade which, with the declining prices of our raw materials on the world market, constitutes one sector that if well exploited, could revive our ailing economy.

Government has spent the last 30 years since independence laying the foundation blocks for a buoyant tourist industry and today we have many tourist attractions to cater for all kinds of tourists. For example, to make the tourist's life less complicated, we decided to build a sprawling slum residential area within the precincts of the five star hotels in our capital city so our visitors don't have to go far to see how we live. And for tourist guides, we have recruited and trained some of this country's well-known linguists who speak a mouthful of languages to line the road leading to the hotels and beg.

The government is painfully aware that our women who should be championing this national cause, have not shown the enthusiasm required of them. We know, for example, that our women are adept at exposing all parts of their body, including their breasts, whether full blown or dangling, but when it comes to exposing the essential part that matters, they hold back. That is not good for the tourist industry. The tourists and visitors definitely need more exposure. The bodies of our women are potential natural resources and we should exploit them.

Some people have argued that unchecked tourism can alter our way of life by exposing our people to alien practices, mores etc. They point to the increase in rampant prostitution in our cities as one of the pernicious effects of tourism, as well as the spread of venereal disease, AIDS, vandalism and drugs. I would be hiding their nakedness with my fingers if I were to disagree with this analysis just as I believe very seriously that AIDS didn't just happen the way scientists want us to believe it happened.

Since civilized society controls the world's media, it wants the world to believe that AIDS started in Africa. My own reasoning is that the dreadful disease escaped from somebody's laboratory or that the virus was tested on our unsuspecting African brothers and sisters since we are usually used as guinea pigs anyway. We hope the criminal will be brought to book and charged with attempted extermination.

I don't think it is fair to blame tourism alone for our people's promiscuous ways. It would be denying that our people are resourceful in their own right. Parents have given up on their children and have allowed them to drift at will in clouds of cigarette and marijuana smoke and drown rivers of alcohol.

It is well known that I established the Ashawo Committee chaired by Mandzah's most famous madam, Mami Ashawo, to study the problem of prostitution and to make suggestions to government. Certainly, government must intervene to regulate the manner in which our prostitutes sleep with their partners. One avenue we are exploring will lead to our allowing the prostitutes to charge customers according to the style and posture adopted during the act. For now, I wouldn't want to bare anything by preempting the committee's recommendations.

It is also well known that when our prostitutes knew that a survey was being conducted, they all congregated, in their best finery, that is naked, in front of the Peoples' House with a petition to government to stop prying into their life. The extremists among them went overboard and accused government of prying into their private parts. Of course, there is no truth to the accusation, and I think our people need to be enlightened on the facts.

Since this government is steadfast in its mission, we decided that, notwithstanding the delaying tactics adopted by these women (we assume that they are all women and not men masquerading as women), the Ashawo Committee should be given a few years within which to submit its findings.

Agriculture

That agriculture is the mainstay of our economy is beyond doubt. It is for this reason that since becoming President, I have not spared any efforts in boosting the agricultural sector by encouraging crop diversification as a way of lifting up our limping economy. I shall not relent in my efforts until we achieve food self-sufficiency. For most African countries, this is an elusive goal, but as far as we in Mandzah are concerned, I pledge, once again, as I did 30 years ago, that food self-sufficiency is within our reach.

I do not think it serves any useful purpose for me to go over the guiding principles of our agricultural policy which has been so successful. I shall simply deal with some of the controversial aspects that have been misunderstood and misrepresented.

Cash crops

Everyone knows that cash crops are the props of the agricultural sector in all African countries. The reason for this state of affairs is obvious. When the white man came to Africa, he developed plantations that would mass-produce the raw materials that their industries back home needed. That is why all our countries produce mainly cash crops of one kind or another. We in Mandzah are lucky that with our climate, we can produce coffee, cocoa, bananas, palm oil, tea, rubber, cotton, pepper, etc. Some countries are not so lucky.

When I became the guide of this nation, I increased the production of these cash crops, but there are many forces working against us, the forces of evil. Over the years, Tubab middlemen and consumers have banded together and signed a blood pact to pay steadily declining prices for our cash crops. The results are there for everyone to see. Our foreign exchange earnings have dropped significantly and we are no longer able to do for our people what we used to do in the past. This too has significantly reduced the standing amount that the government used to transfer to my personal national bank accounts abroad to save for the rainy day.

We have appealed to our Tubab friends to be understanding in these times of economic crisis. We continue to pledge our loyalty to them, supporting them in the face of widespread world condemnation, but their government maintains that it cannot intervene in the market place and that market forces determine prices. Yet they continue to give subsidies to their farmers to compete against us.

As long as African countries do not develop an industrial base; as long as we do not develop industries to transform our raw materials into semi-finished or finished goods, we shall continue to depend on the whims of the Tubab consumer. No nation can survive this way.

The Tubabs buy our raw materials for nothing and sell us the processed products for horrendously high prices that we cannot afford. And we are expected to pay for this in hard currency that we do not have.

In the face of this serious problem, I set up a task force five years ago under the chairmanship of the venerable Dr. Koyimi, one of Mandzah's foremost herbalists and native doctors, to look at the issue critically and make recommendations to the government. It was the government's understanding that since Dr. Koyimi knows plants well, he will also know edible plants or, what some people call food crops. We were not wrong.

The Koyimi Task Force submitted a detailed report on its findings three years ago, and government is still studying its recommendations. At the time we commissioned the study, we did not know that we were dealing with a complicated subject since we see plants growing everywhere in Mandzah. We have appointed a 10-man committee to look into the report of the Koyimi Task Force and to report to government as soon as possible within the next five years.

Food crops

Any nation that cannot feed itself is a sick nation. That is why my government has encouraged the diversification of our agricultural base. We are flattered that other countries look at us with envy and praise us for having a sound agricultural policy. It is to the credit of this government that none of our citizens goes to bed hungry at night. Thank God, the abhorrent scenes that are depicted on television screens the world over everyday of starving children were not shot in Mandzah. My people must pay deserved tribute to our party and to me, its standard-bearer and chairman.

However, notwithstanding our efforts to attain food self-sufficiency, we must deplore the fact that some of our citizens who do not have the interest of our people at heart, continue to conspire to sell food across our territorial borders to earn foreign exchange. This is sabotage of the economy and I have served them notice that if they are caught, we shall treat them like traitors. It is not normal that food should be so expensive in this country when we produce all of it here.

We do have some problems, however. As it is generally known, many foodstuffs such as wheat and rice used to be consumed irregularly in this country. Today, their consumption has increased by leaps and bounds and the government has been forced to resort to massive imports to meet local demand. Several reasons account for this: burgeoning town and city population, newly acquired taste, ease of storage and preparation, etc.

We have stepped up our rice production and should soon achieve rice self-sufficiency. While the government is straining under the weight of so many problems and doing its level best to solve them, detractors continue to accuse it of foot-dragging and pussyfooting. But we have not been sleeping.

We have recently entered an agreement whereby the United Conquerors Republic will grant us, under their TI (Trade Intensification) program, a credit of $20 million to purchase rice from them. This means that we will allow the United Conquerors

Republic and other countries to flood our markets with dirt-cheap and very poor quality rice that their pigs refuse to eat. We in the government believe the agreement is in our favour and my government stands to gain a lot from it. If we do not purchase the rice United Conquerors Republic farmers will riot and cause problems for President Jim John Jones Jack Jr. who has always stood by us. Our detractors should understand that we are also contributing to strengthening the United Conquerors Republic economy and by extension world peace. We are adverse to waste and cannot stand the sight of United Conquerors Republic farmers and their government dumping rice in the ocean because it cannot be sold or because it is of such inferior quality that even their animals will not eat it. We say they should dump it on us. After all, what are friends for?

Another benefit accruing to my government from this rice agreement with its generous terms is that this government stands to make lots of money from it because the rice will be sold at a reasonably high price on our local market. Since we already have a long list of government and party cronies who have applied to obtain licences to sell the rice wholesale, there will be no problem with marketing it.

After the various government officials responsible for signing the papers for the importation of the rice have received their own share of the money, the rest of the funds are transferred to my personal national account abroad as savings for the rainy day. Knowing how greedy our people are, and the length to which they can go to swindle government, I and I alone have access to the personal national bank account.

Our detractors have harped on the fact that this agreement will depress local rice production because imported rice will flood our markets and compete with our locally produced rice. These detractors are behind time and trying to close the pig fence after the pig has bolted. Any observer can see that imported rice has already flooded our markets and that that is precisely what our consumers want.

People should understand that the agreement with the United Conquerors Republic has generous terms for us. First, we do not have to come up with the money immediately. Second, rice will always be available on our market, thus staving off not only hunger but also riots. Thirdly, we make so much money on the imported rice that the key government officials and rice dealers will kill me if I tried to disband rice imports.

Of course, it is true that imported rice will depress local rice production and block our path to rice self-sufficiency. That is true but it does not matter. We will be self-sufficient in imported rice since we will have enough rice on the market. Socio-economic surveys undertaken by our National Institute for Food Substitutes (NIFS) show that, at the rate at which our people are consuming imported foodstuffs and drinking foreign wines and alcohol, Mandzah should be self-sufficient in these imports in the next five years.

The NIFS, which is one of Mandzah's premier research institutions, was set up last year by government to carry out research on potential imported foodstuff that may eventually replace our local foodstuff. The results so far obtained are very promising as far as rice, maize, millet, sorghum and all the cereals we produce are concerned. We hope the institute will double its ration and take on research on tropical fruits such as oranges, pineapples, avocado, and mango, guava that we grow abundantly. The earlier we stop producing these products and rely on massive imports as has been the case with wheat and rice, the better will be the financial situation of those to whom government has issued import licences.

In the light of the foregoing scientific and economic analysis, no one should take the bedraggled band of perpetual dissidents that has been campaigning for my government to ban rice imports seriously. They are jealous that imported rice is giving a lot of us in government a lot of money, and that if we do the same thing to the other foodstuffs, we would be billionaires while they are left out of the feast.

The view of this government is that local rice production will not put money in the government's coffers. People must understand that the imported rive gives quite a lot of money and consolidates the already excellent ties we have with the United Conquerors Republic. It is a symbiotic relationship. The United Conquerors Republic farmers are happy that instead of dumping their rice in the sea and getting nothing for it, they are able to dump it on us and make lots of money from it. Our consumers are happy that rice is readily available on the local market and that they don't have to go for the locally produced, more nutritious rice that our people toil to produce under very difficult conditions every year. Government too is happy because as long as our people have rice in their mouths, they cannot shout and scream.

Instead of appreciating government's foresight, the voices of evil have been clamouring for my head. They claim that we are stockpiling local rice and other foodstuffs so as to create artificial shortages and thus justify continued imports that pump money into our pockets. I don't think any government in its right mind will prefer to store these foodstuffs and feed rats, cockroaches and beetles instead of its citizens. I say this because we all know that all the warehouses around the country are infested with these pests.

By the time our own locally produced rice is on the market, it is already damaged. We have therefore been stockpiling our local produce not to create shortages but to ensure that all the imported food items our people need are sold. We do not want our local food crops to compete with our food imports.

At the same time that we are promoting the rice trade of our United Conquerors Republic friends, we are also encouraging agricultural research in our country in all fields: rice, cocoyam, cassava, yams, beans, millet, sorghum, etc. Food self-sufficiency remains our main goal, and we shall not rest until we have achieved it. To this end, we have welcomed into our country several agricultural research organizations interested in helping us to reach our goal. This is one area in which international cooperation is absolutely essential.

My government is fully committed to agricultural research as can be seen from the myriads of research institutes we have established since independence. It is true that may of them are idle because they do not have facilities and because the key scientific staff have fled the country as a result of atrocious working conditions. The Ngwashi Commission found out that some unscrupulous scientists and researchers had sold some of the equipment, and that the minister of technology transfer and adaptation (formerly minister of scientific research and technology generation) had decided to sell what was left so that the government would not lose everything. As soon as we receive the aid we requested from our foreign friends, we should be in a position to order new equipment, recruit new staff, and, hopefully, begin research in earnest.

Unfortunately, most people do not understand that research is expensive and time-consuming. It takes a very long time for major research breakthroughs to be made. We should be patient.

The Ngwashi Commission expressed misgivings about the type of research being conducted by the international agricultural research institutions working in Africa and the Third World. According to the Commission, these institutions are conducting high-tech research the results of which cannot readily be adopted by our farmers. The Commission goes on to say that the technologies these international research institutes are experimenting with are imported and not adapted to our farmers' conditions.

This government considers these allegations to be very serious charges that could undermine the basis of our research cooperation agreements with Tubab countries as a whole. I have therefore set up the Pa Nyamka Committee to look into the report of the Ngwashi Committee and to report to me. Pa Nyamka's Committee has a broad mandate to review our entire agricultural research policy and to make recommendations to government. I am very confident that the Committee will make appropriate suggestions.

Pa Nyamka should bring to the Committee the wealth of experience he has acquired over the years from the strategic positions he occupied in this country before his retirement. He used to be the chief night watchman in the then ministry of research and technology generation for over thirty years before being promoted to the key and instrumental position of chief clerk in the same ministry. As chief night watchman, Pa Nyamka was responsible for guarding all our country's research findings. On the recommendation of the minister of research and technology generation, Pa Nyamka was promoted to the key position of chief clerk *emeritus* after he successfully foiled a plan by a few burglars to break into our laboratories to steal some of this country's most prized research instruments – a wheel barrow, empty bottles and a second-hand tyre.

The Pa Nyamka Committee has also been mandated to confirm reports that the majority of the Tubabs working in our research institutions come to Mandzah primarily to make money and to undertake research to enable them write research papers to ensure their academic promotion when they return to their respective countries.

Without jumping to conclusions on the results of the Committee, we know that the bulk of the research budget is used to pay the salaries and fringe benefits of these foreign researchers under the pretext that our research institutions must be competitive internationally. I say that is hogwash because I have yet to be told of any foreign researcher in Mandzah who, because of their original research, won an international prize. Like in business and the other fields, it is safe to say that the Tubab experts that come to our country do so because of the money. How many of them would earn what they are earning if they remained in their country?

The Committee should also look into allegations that our farmers have been persistently refusing to adopt many of the agricultural techniques developed by these institutions and that foreign researchers come into our country to subjugate us to research bondage.

Education

Education is one of my government's greatest priorities. We cannot develop as a people if we are lacking in education. Our continent has been given names because we lag behind in education and come at the end of the development race. We need trained manpower in all fields to help with the task of nation building. My government is acutely aware of this and has made the construction of schools throughout the country its greatest concern. In the area of education, we have developed a number of policy options that we intend to adhere to rigidly.

Primary School

Unless we start preparing our children in their young age for future national responsibilities, we shall not make any meaningful progress. Accordingly, we shall ensure that more schools are built and that the best education is given to our children. The minister of education, illiteracy and re-education has proposed that our children be taught civics lesson so that they grow up to be responsible citizens. I have made this the keystone of our educational policy.

Our children will spend half the time studying my philosophical works and the rest of the time other ancillary disciplines. Once a week, they will undertake military drills to learn how to defend their country, and attend the party school once a month for indoctrination lessons.

Secondary School

There is widespread grumbling that there are not enough secondary schools for our rapidly growing student population. I think we need to thank the missions for their continued assistance in this crucial sector. Like in the case of the primary schools, we shall build more schools, and offer advance philosophical and indoctrination classes.

I recall that secondary school teachers have been restless over the last few years. They have always complained that their salaries are low and not paid on time, that their working conditions are very poor, and that it seems government has neglected them. I wish to assuage them that this government does not neglect any of its citizenry. Our commitment to the welfare of all our citizens is unshakable.

We also would want to plead with all the teachers to put their students on a leash. We cannot tolerate lawlessness nor can students be allowed to arrogate to themselves the right to go on strike at will. When the teachers' delegation met with us at the table of negotiations two years ago, we agreed that if they hold the students in check from embarrassing government, we would look into their grievances. We stand by that solemn promise.

University

We recognize that our national university is small and have cut the sod for the building of an agricultural and technical university in Mamben. It is our hope that those who will be admitted to this new university will be more mature than their counterparts in the National University who have made demonstrations and strikes their pastime.

In the area of higher education, our Higher Education Council chaired by Hon. Tamti, former Member of Parliament and now a peasant farmer in his home village of Mben, has drawn up new syllabuses for most of the courses. One of the noteworthy changes is that we shall prevent students from going abroad to undertake courses that are available at our National University.

For the peace and harmony of our country, we have also deemed it expedient to lay down certain guidelines that the university administration and students are called upon to respect scrupulously. The newly appointed vice-chancellor, Prof. Wetingcall Naweman, knows the university well since he served first as dean of the faculty of political education before being appointed as permanent secretary in the ministry of raw materials and commodities, a position he served concurrently with that of propaganda director of our national party.

Prof. Wetingcall Naweman was appointed to the university position to cool tempers that are always flaring between students and the government. In his position as propaganda director of our party, Prof. Naweman defended government policy well and set up a very efficient spy network on the university campus to keep tabs on dissident students in the opposition. The government hopes that he will be able to do more now that he will be much closer to the students.

The first bold measure Prof. Naweman took was to declare that henceforth there would no longer be any orientation at the National University. We believe that incoming students are mature enough to decide for themselves what they want to do. If upon graduation they do not have jobs, they will be able to work in the attractive unemployment sector and not blame government. To date, we have over 15,000 graduates in law, the liberal arts and social sciences enjoying their enviable unemployment position and living off their parents and friends. Add to that the increasing number of doctors, engineers, architects, scientists etc.

The issue of unemployment is one that has serious repercussions on our economy, and thus on the stability of our country. In other words, employment is correlated with stability in direct proportion to the correlation of unemployment with instability. If we deprive strike-prone students of jobs after graduation, they will become subservient, self-seeking patriots. The longer we keep people out of jobs, the easier it is to break their will and make them put their party, government, country and revered leaser first. Unemployment is therefore a tactical weapon that we have fought to acquire.

We have temporarily stopped hiring graduates in keeping with the order given by the International Union of Money Changers. Foreign consultants will man the key sectors of our economy that require trained manpower. All government ministries, state-owned corporations, churches, private companies and embassies have been ordered to stop hiring nationals. As our economy improves, we shall resume hiring on the basis of the list prepared by my office.

For the unemployment policy to be well implemented, we have had to establish, at great financial cost to our people, a special elite corps to monitor the activities of all our students at home and abroad. This elite corps routinely recruits girls to spy on their colleagues.

Teachers

Outside the home, teachers exercise the greatest influence on our children who are tomorrow's adults. Teachers are responsible for giving our children the educational foundation that will mould them into law-abiding and hard-working citizens. This is no mean responsibility and my government recognizes that without good, dedicated teachers, our children will not develop into the good citizens that we all expect.

As much as we all realize that our teachers are in the cockpit of the development process, we believe they must also set the example for our children to follow. Our teachers must serve as role models and do as they preach because our children are watching and copying them. But what do we see? Every school year our teachers lay down their chalk and forward a laundry list of grievances to the minister of education, illiteracy and re-education with an ultimatum that if government doesn't pay attention to their litany of woes, they will walk out of class for good.

We acknowledge that some of the teachers' grievances are justified, but we cannot understand why teachers resort to threats and strikes whenever they want a dialogue with government. That obviously is not a civilized way of trying to resolve an issue.

We know that these problems have been around since independence, and believe it is in the interest of the teachers, the government and our children for me to outline what my government is going to do about them.

The first thing is for the teachers to drop any remote thought they might have of going on strike. Maybe they do not realize the extent to which a teachers' strike disrupts the life of this nation. During a strike, there are no classes and the teachers appear to be playing truant. That obviously is not good for them or the children.

Secondly, I do not buy the argument that teachers are poorly paid. They only have to look at their colleagues in the unemployment sector to see what I mean. Most of our teachers are in the rural areas where they are in fact spoiled. School children provide them with firewood while parents provide them with food. Also, life is far cheaper than in the city. They walk and do not have to worry about taxis since there are no taxis or motorable roads. Furthermore, thy do not have to worry about paying electricity, water, and telephone bills since these facilities do not exist. I therefore fail to see their point.

In the light of what I have just said, I am serving notice to our teachers that my government has shown tremendous equanimity under the stressful conditions caused by the teachers. They have a duty before history to ensure that this nation produces the best citizens of the future. Surely this is a more noble calling than roaming the streets everyday with placards calling for higher salaries, an improvement in working conditions, firing of the minister of education, illiteracy and re-education, etc.

University teaching staff

My understanding when our National University was opened a few years after independence was that we would be able to mass-produce our own scientists, technicians and professionals in the various fields. Initially we were on target. We started with the departments of Sanskrit, Latin, Greek, Hebrew, and Indo-European Languages that we needed badly for our development.

As funds became available, we entered into a twinning relationship with the University of Lonlong and expanded our programs to include the fields that all developing countries think they need as a matter of urgency such as English, French Language and Civilization, German, Spanish, Portuguese, Law, History,

Sociology and Political Science. A few years ago, we decided to expand further and introduced a few science subjects such as Mathematics, Physics, Biology and Chemistry.

I think we can rightfully be proud of the tremendous progress that our National University has made. The next decade should be a period of challenge as our scientists compete favourably with their colleagues from other universities.

The Nobel Prize has eluded us for too long and, allowing for the hard conditions under which we know our students have been working without well-equipped laboratories and other facilities, we are sure that the medical doctors graduating from our Biology department, the nuclear physicists from the Physics department and the astronauts from the Chemistry department are comparable with their colleagues anywhere in the world.

It was also my understanding that our university faculty would be made up of men and women steeped in the lore of learning. Again, in this area, we cannot complain as we have some of the best brains in the world. We are faithful to our commitments. Every year our university recruits some of the best foreign lecturers that come to our country to do their master's degree research. Since a university is a place for the cross-fertilization of ideas, we believe that our students will benefit from such international exposure.

I do not know of any group in this country as privileged as our university teaching staff. The vice-chancellor has informed me that most of them teach a maximum of four hours a day. At first I was angry because I thought this was done intentionally to match my own working hours, but the vice-chancellor explained that the university teaching staff need the other four hours to prepare their lessons, mark papers, and conduct research.

I find nothing wrong with this because that is precisely what I do. I spend four hours lecturing my ministers and receiving dignitaries, and the four hours preparing my lectures for the following day. However, unlike the university teaching staff, I spend the rest of the time doing research on who is planning a coup. I must say I spend sleepless nights poring over security briefing papers, listening to foreign radio broadcasts to learn what they are saying about my government, reading books written by false writers and articles in newspapers and magazines we have banned from entering this country. I design development schemes, listen to gossip and so on and so forth. The results of my research are usually published in the form of long, breathtaking speeches and decrees or read on national radio and television every night.

It is in recognition of these scholarly publications and my outstanding contribution to the arts, sciences and technology that several universities in the world have been begging me to accept the conferment on me of *honoris causa* degrees. So far I have received nine such degrees from some of the world's most prestigious universities. It is indeed an honour for my young country that I should be considered by the world's intellectual community as deserving of such high academic honours.

Every coin has its head and tail just as every country has its patriots and traitors. Our country's traitors have been telling the world that because I have lots of money and fame, I usually buy *honoris causa* degrees. I am not aware that these degrees are on the market although I know that they are awarded to every Tom, Dick and Harry.

How can one explain the fact that just as the Saint Lazarus University was awarding me one such degree, the Native People's University was awarding one to President Ntambeng of Alankyi whom everyone knows to be a kleptomaniac, murderer, and dictator of the first order? I am not surprised because I know how some of these so-called institutions of higher learning or, to use the expression in vogue, centres of excellence, operate.

There are countless other universities which have been beckoning to me to accept their degrees and I have been refusing. They want to use my name and popularity to enhance their own image. And they think that because of their free degree, I will give them money. I am not a fool because if I were one, I wouldn't be considered by the international community as some big intellectual.

Having said this, and considering the similarity in my role of President and that of the university teaching staff, I find it totally unacceptable that the university teaching staff should spend the little time they have criticizing government. I don't criticize government and do not see why they should.

One would have expected that as the intellectuals they say they are, they would channel their criticisms to their disciplines and leave politics to politicians. Instead what do we see? They spend more time criticizing government and witch-hunting than doing research. Each of them wants to be head of department, dean or vice-chancellor. They do not understand that academic qualifications alone are not enough and that teaching positions, like all other senior positions in government, go with a certain degree of political maturity.

Notwithstanding their great learning, and maybe because of it, these university teaching staff do not seem capable of proposing suitable solutions to national problems. If the time they spend in bars were computed, most of them would get A + + for alcoholism and 0 - - for research. They are vocal when it comes to criticizing and accusing my government of nepotism, but we all know that female students who refuse to stoop to their animal instincts always fail to graduate. These are the so-called intellectuals who want to lead Mandzah.

I do not want to bare our university faculty but because of their persistently subjective and farfetched criticisms of my government, I think the world is entitled to know the truth. In their last petition to me for higher salaries and allowances, they complained that most Mandzah graduates refuse to return home because of the high unemployment rate, low salaries and poor working conditions. We all know this is to be true because our policy is to discourage the employment of our graduates and to create conditions that are most conducive for unemployment.

Our university faculty is advised, in its own interest, to stick to what it knows how to do best, namely over-indulge in alcohol and sex, serve as errand boys for Tubab researchers, write rave reviews about my publications and ask students for bribes if they want to pass. They should leave government alone because they do not know anything about governing.

Furthermore, when one looks at our National University, it is patently obvious that very little research is taking place there. When one considers that there is so much about our country that we know so little about, one wonders why every graduating student is not requested to write a thesis or graduating paper on a topic of local or national interest in their field. The bulk of what is published on Mandzah is published by Tubabs, some of who come to our country as tourists and then turn out to be the world's foremost experts on our country.

Considering the declining standards in our university, I, in my capacity as Chancellor of the National University of Mandzah, decided that the following measures should be implemented with immediate effect:

1. All final year students are to submit a research paper in their field on a topic that deals with their village, tribe, ethnic group or country. No exoteric topic will be entertained. We are sick and tired of reading, for example, about Napoleon, the royal families and all the other Tubab heroes. Why hasn't any one written about me? I am sure I can be the object of a devastatingly damaging psychological, sociological, historical, cultural, and medical treatise.
2. Promotion of faculty members at the National University will be based on productivity. All university teaching staff must write at least one original research paper on a local topic before they can be considered for promotion. Tenure will be based on the quality of research publications.
3. University teaching staff may continue to get drunk during working hours like all their compatriots in government. We cannot deprive our people of their little pleasures. However, strikes, demonstrations and sit-ins are banned.
4. Government recognizes the difficulty in regulating social behaviour. Nevertheless, a university faculty member accused of mating with a female student will be summarily dismissed, turned over to the ministry of justice, trials and imprisonment for prosecution, and imprisoned for at least 10 years.
5. University faculty members who exhibit exemplary conduct by writing positive things about the government and exposing their colleagues who criticize the government will be allowed to go on sabbatical and study leave on full salary.

Foreign Affairs

I have tried in my public life to maintain extremely cordial relations with all my colleagues. In fact, the touchstone of our policy is peaceful coexistence with every nation, irrespective of whether we like the leader or not. Leaders come and go but the people remain, although they can be exterminated, purified, or cleansed.

His Excellency Tchatcha Merengue

I know the reader will want to know why I closed the border with neighbouring Leka three years ago. The facts of the matter are very simple. We had a meeting in Tsugeboh, capital of Mandzah, to which all the heads of state of neighbouring countries were invited, including President Tchatcha Merengue of Leka. Before the meeting ended, one of my ubiquitous security officers pinched me and said Merengue's foreign minister, Nicodemus Joshua Lekumbeng, was fidgeting with my youngest daughter, Bih Lemoh Mangye.

I called Bih and talked to her like a father would to his daughter. Bih assured me that she would put an end to the alleged romance. Before I realized it, the foreign minister had eloped with my daughter and returned to Jika even before the end of the meeting. I called my colleague, President Merengue, and protested to him vehemently about what his foreign minister had done.

You know what Merengue said? That he did not feel that he should meddle in the private life of his foreign minister; that my daughter was a consenting adult since she was at the time 27, and that since Mr. Nicodemus Joshua Lekumbeng was single, my daughter might just have been the type of woman he was looking for. Then he added that whatever punishment he was going to mete out to his foreign minister for abandoning an official meeting did not concern me.

I fired off a note of protest to Merengue in which I said I believed his foreign minister had not only interfered in my country's internal affairs but very likely in my daughter's private parts. I added that I had been reserving my daughter for a head of state and not for a mere foreign minister.

Merengue took offence at my letter and refused to cooperate in returning my daughter. I had no other choice but to declare a state of emergency and close our common border.

Who, by the way, is Tchatcha Merengue, and why should he refuse to cooperate with me? But for me, Merengue would have been overthrown many times because opponents of his government use my country as a staging area. Had I given them the support they requested, Merengue wouldn't have been around for his lunatic foreign minister to be tampering with my daughter. Furthermore, because Leka depends on us entirely for food, we can send them to sudden and instantaneous death overnight if we ban our food exports into his country. This I refused to do on ethical grounds because I believe that Merengue's people have nothing to do with his lunacy. Lastly, my country provides unlimited job opportunities to Lekans and if we want to choke Leka's economy, all we have to do is expel all Lekans as some of our neighbouring countries have taken pleasure in doing.

The world knows that two years ago, Lekans were expelled by President Anyo of neighbouring Ebebechere out of jealousy because Lekans are very enterprising and prosperous. We in Mandzah have never given in to such temptation because we believe fervently in African unity and integration. But there are limits to how much we can stomach from Merengue. He should have known that playing with me is like playing with fire.

I would like history to know that as much as we are willing to cooperate with all peace-loving people the world over, we shall be uncompromising in the defence of our territorial integrity. We cannot allow any country to interfere in our internal affairs with impunity, and get away with it.

His Excellency Idimina Abominabo

World leaders watched with horror and blood pact complacency the rise and fall of Idimina Abominabo, the mischievous dictator who glorified Hitler's name. It wasn't until he fell from power that the world awoke to the horrors he had committed, much like it did when Hitler held sway over Europe. That is the folly of the world. We too often show collective weakness in the face of incipient tyranny. We never react until the cancer has become fatal to our body politic.

My government, like all world governments, maintained ties with Abominabo's government in the hope that refusing to ostracize him would soften him. Hasn't the world tried all that with dictators and fascist regimes and failed? But we were not alone. Abominado maintained close ties with all civilized countries, and they supplied him with all the arms he needed to wield absolute power over his people. While Tubabs, for all their vociferous condemnations of dictatorships, overthrow left-leaning regimes, they wine and dine with murderous right-wing butchers.

His Excellency Leshure Weshune

It is true that my country has had a long-standing cold relationship with neighbouring Njinmambang. This is understandable. From time immemorial, we have appealed to Weshume to stem the tide of his country's migrants who stray into our country looking for job opportunities, but to no avail. We have even said at the United People's Meeting that we subscribe to the doctrine of free movement of peoples. At the same time we have said that our neighbours' territory should not be used by those of our misguided citizens fleeing from justice.

Weshune has continued, despite our protests, to give refuge and a sanctuary to our enemies. The banned so-called People's Revolutionary Movement has bases in Njinmambang. We have firm evidence that the attacks of which our peaceful and peace-loving citizens are victims have been aided and abetted by Weshune.

Efforts to convince him to stop giving these fellows military assistance and sanctuary have failed. We have therefore served notice that we would retaliate by expelling all his nationals from our country for espionage.

By the way, who are the ringleaders of the so-called People's Revolutionary Movement? First, there is Nyamkala who served as my personal adviser on economic affairs for over twenty-five years. When he was denounced in the abortive fake coup trial last year, he escaped to Njinmambang and Weshune gave him sanctuary. He has been telling the world that I have ruined the economy; that I have embezzled aid funds; that I have amassed a personal fortune exceeding the gross domestic product of my country and so many evil lies. And the world believes him. No one is asking how come all this was happening when he was my adviser on economic affairs.

Second, there is Captain Ekwed, the rebel soldier whom I freed from the gallows even though I received numerous petitions to hang him. Today he is a free man and believes he can use his inside knowledge of our military establishment to betray my country. I say he is a traitor. He is not a soldier but a coward. He claims that I sent the army to raze an entire village because the villagers did not vote for me in the presidential elections of some years ago. But everybody knows that I got 106.63% in those elections, which means that everybody voted for me, including a select group of dead people.

How can Ekwed then go round telling the world that I slaughtered my own people in cold blood when they all voted for me? The lie is so palpable, but no one seems to be questioning why if he were the exemplary soldier that he now claims to be, he executed my commands. Assuming that it is true that I gave the orders for the entire village to be razed to the ground, why did he not refuse and go underground as he has done now if he thought I was wrong? These are criminals who are running away with the blood of their fellow countrymen on their hands. Their treachery will catch up with them someday.

Third, there is Mandooh Wumu. He was my minister of finance, pre-finance, debts and liquidation for seventeen years. It is not a lie that Wumu was a very inefficient minister. He was the architect of our Five Year Underdevelopment Plans that won acclaim worldwide within the donor community. Under Wumu, the economy was strengthened as the International Lenders Association poured money into Mandzah. We were courted left and right to get loans we did not need, and unemployment was very high.

In the process of doing all this good work, Wumu also built up a huge foreign bank account for himself rivalling mine. We must all admit that there can only be one president in the country. It was most irreverent of Wumu to compete with me in taking money abroad. Each time I asked him to transfer money into my personal national bank account abroad, he would also transfer an equivalent amount to his own account. I pretended that I did not know what was happening because one cannot rub the chief's back with palm oil and then wipe one's hands on the ground. This was the way things were done and I had to close my eyes to some of these things.

Things got to a head two years ago when we went to attend the African Solidarity Summit meeting in Ngamatog. Wumu and I had agreed that we would need a suitcase of crisp $100 bills to foot the bills of my country's delegation. The 747 presidential aircraft was going to take me, my spouse and children, some members of the government, and key military officers. Experience from other African countries shows that a president must be a real fool to venture out of the country without taking along all key military officers.

To my greatest dismay, when we reached Ngamatog and checked into our presidential suite, Wumu absconded with the money, ran to Tubab and was immediately granted political asylum. I later on learned that he had spirited away about $1.7 million. To cover up his tracks, he said he was fleeing political repression at home. We do not have any evidence that the Tubab customs, immigration officers and banks ever queried how one man could be travelling with so much money on him. Only drug money seems to have a foul smell.

We also have proof that Wumu ripped this country off in other ways but we have tried unsuccessfully to extradite him to come and face trial for his economic crimes. Instead, the mass media in Tubab pours out a steady stream of destabilizing news about my country. Instead of helping us to catch this master thief, every day the story is the same: President Wan Nei of Mandzah is corrupt; he is autocratic; he is muzzling the press; he is this and that. No one seems to be seeing all the good work I am doing.

I say my power comes from the people and the day they say they are fed up with me, I shall hang my gloves and boots. I was freely elected life-President, and the Tubabs are jealous because in their own countries, presidents are so weak that they come and go.

All of us African presidents are strong and tough because we have the people on our side and it is not people like Wumu and Co. that will stand in the way of our national edification process.

Lastly, there is Florence Nyanga, the whore who is as promiscuous as my dogs and rabbits. The world is forgetting that I was one of the first, if not the first African president, to give full meaning to the doctrine of equal rights for the sexes. I do not say this in any particularly paternalistic way. The truth is that even before white women started clamouring for the right to be like men, I had already recognized that the Mandzah woman had all the characteristics of his male counterpart. I, against the grain of popular sentiment, single-handedly amended the constitution to give our women voting rights. I enshrined in my country's constitution respect for the woman and for womanhood.

At the convention of our popular and democratic party, even before the eyes of the rest of Africans were opened to the eclipse of colonialism, I championed the cause of the woman. Some evil minds have said I crusaded for the rights of women because I did not know my own mother; because my father had used my mother and ran away, and because I was a womaniser. I say history will tell because we in Mandzah know a woman when we see one.

Who was Florence Nyanga? This was a whore that I dug out of flophouses, rehabilitated, and appointed to key positions in my cabinet. She had absolutely no education, and had been the playmate of the Tubab soldiers stationed in Afofo, our coastal city. I made her my minister of women's affairs (although she behaved as if she was in charge of men's affairs), then minister of health, hospitalisation and death. The last post she occupied was that of minister of social welfare.

It was in this last position that Nyanga betrayed me, the party and her country. She took her position too seriously and misunderstood what social welfare means. She started throwing her weight around, throwing her body to every Tom, Dick and Harry, especially to every dick, foreign diplomats in this country, and even some of my ministers. This was most dishonourable for a minister. The country nicknamed her Florence Night Angel. I fell ashamed. I alone was supposed to know what her body looked like, not the entire nation.

Enough is enough. I called Nyanga to my office many times and drew her attention to the scandal she was causing my government. There was even talk that she was passing secrets to one of the foreign diplomats she was throwing her body to, but I do not have any evidence of that.

In order to remove the shame that she was causing her husband, a lowly paid civil servant, I decided to appoint Mr. Nyanga as an ambassador. Rumours were rife that I had appointed Mr. Nyanga abroad so I could have his wife to myself.

The fact is that I did this in the hope that since absence makes the heart grow fonder, Mrs. Nyanga would miss her husband and so behave better. I could have easily eliminated Mr. Nyanga if I had wanted to and no one would have raised their little finger. Mr. Nyanga would not have been the first or the last person that I have eliminated. I recall that one student was made to disappear because he persisted in seeing a girlfriend that my protocol people had brought to me.

In any case, I was wrong that Mr. Nyanga's absence would make Mrs. Nyanga's heart grow fonder. A whore is a whore is a whore. Mrs. Nyanga indulged even more in her own brand of social welfare work. I decided to sack her, but wanted a propitious moment to do so without disgracing her.

Somehow Mrs. Nyanga learned about my plans, or suspected that I wouldn't put up with her very long, all the more as I had warned her several times. She invented a mission abroad, resigned and joined her former bed partners abroad in smearing the name of her president and her country. I do not want to give undue importance to the hallucinations of a whore by bothering to respond to all the incredibly irresponsible things she has been saying both in print and on the air about me, my government, and my people.

I hear she is writing a book. An illiterate, like me, writing a book. If she is writing from the diary she kept as a whore, I sure would be delighted to read it. I have heard that she is now working for the Tubab secret police department. I don't doubt that she will bare them someday since baring is her might.

His Excellency Jim John Jones Jack Jr.

We are unwavering in our attachment to democracy and democratic ideals. We shall not compromise on any principles that infringe on human rights. It therefore goes without saying that we share the same political and humanistic view of the world as President Jim John Jones Jack Jr. of the United Conquerors Republic.

Those who oppose our worldview, closet revolutionaries and their ilk, point to President Jim Jack Jr.'s paternalistic arrogance and refusal to bail us out, especially in the present world economic crisis. They do not understand that democracy and capitalism do not necessarily go hand in hand.

I have been around long enough, and have met with almost every significant world leader. President Jim Jack Jr., though extremely young, is ahead of his time. He is probably one of the few leaders who clearly understands that our one world is inextricably linked and that , as long as our continent is rife with economic stagnation, political ferment, and social strife, his own people will never have peace of mind. We are, so to speak, like millstones around their neck.

In terms of foreign aid, we have gained more from our friendship with the United Conquerors Republic than we can ever gain from any other Tubab country. We have a standing annual credit to purchase their rice; we obtain almost all our imports from them on concessionary terms; they intervene at all levels for us to obtain whatever loans we request; they purchase almost all our cash crops and, because of our friendship, we allow them to fix the price.

They helped set up and train our presidential guard, and I must add, still fund it, and lend many other invaluable services. In return, the only thing they are asking us to do is to allow them maintain a well fortified military presence in our country and to use part of our large national territory to dump their stockpiles of waste and also to use our oceans to test their bombs.

It is the view of my government that any sober-minded person who makes a dollar and cent analysis of this privileged two-way relationship will conclude that the United Conquerors Republic has come a cropper on this one.

I said earlier that some people do not understand Tubab philosophy. I do. If people just look around them, they will realize that democracy and capitalism are not necessarily correlated. All the talk about democracy is hot air and baloney. It is true that the Tubabs are democratic but they have never really cared if we are really democratic as they are. All they want us to do is give the world the impression that we are democratic. Proof is that they do not welcome any democratically elected government whose ideology is different from their own. Another thing to remember is that Tubabs are capitalists and that they will defend this system at any cost. Money means more to them than democracy. Any African head of state that understands this will live long. I do.

In fact, most people have wondered about my longevity in power. It is true that I have a tough medicine man that can detect my potential enemies even before they are born. Tubab presidents look at stars to tell them the same thing. But that s not all. I have never made the mistake of not organizing elections since I have nothing to fear.

People do not understand that one can organize an election and ensure one's victory while losing. Our Tubab friends want us to organize elections but they do not care if we stuff ballot boxes or if we post our own people at polling booths to intimidate voters to vote for us. The important thing as far as they are concerned is that we should organize elections and so give the world a semblance of democracy.

President Jim Jack Jr. has been in the vanguard defending my government against false accusations of corruption, human rights violations, and tribalism. He is a friend indeed because he is grateful to us for the little favours we have been doing to him and his people. When he wanted to attack our foulmouthed neighbours, we gave his armed forces the right to refuel over our territory; when other African countries raised the issue of reparations for the slave trade, we stood up against it in support of President Jack Jr. because it was our view that we shouldn't rub red pepper in festering wounds; when his government contacted us to allow them bury their nuclear and other waste in our country, we readily accepted it although some research organizations tried to discourage us by saying that our people might in the long run suffer radiation and water poisoning. We accepted the waste because we need the money in the short run since we know we won't be around in the long run.

When the United Conquerors Republic says anything stupid in international fora, we support them fully and give firm instructions to our representative to go along with everything it says. When many African countries protested to the UCR for invading the People's Republic of Ndongwefor, we were the only African country to stand up and be counted among Tubab countries that supported the UCR.

Notwithstanding all the help we have been giving President Jim Jack Jr. and the people of the United Conquerors Republic, the world press, especially the uncensored Tubab press, has been up in arms against me for my alleged barbaric human rights record. Let me say frankly that the press can say anything it wants. I have the support of the people of the United Conquerors Republic, their parliament and President Jim Jack Jr. The United Conquerors Republic has never said we Africans should not oppress our people. They know that a little oppression of our people is a good and necessary thing, but they want it to be done humanely. Moreover, as long as a government is capitalist and has not adopted a foreign ideology (read my lips, I mean a communist ideology), it is allowed to do anything it can to remain in power. Tubabs usually turn a blind eye to their Third World allies who routinely indulge in a little oppression. This is the secret of my political longevity.

A look round the world will show that those of us who have been hanging around for long are doing so by the grace of our foreign friends. But I do not want to be misunderstood. Tubabs are Tubabs are Tubabs, and one must eat with them with a long spoon. The day Tubabs decide that they no longer need you or, if they sense that you are no longer doing as they have been commanding you to do, you are finished. This is the policy of "noriegation".

During my last state visit to the United Conquerors Republic early this year, amidst all the hoopla about what the press has dubbed my autocratic rule, Jim Jack Jr. told his people that my country is a friend of his and that he thought I was handling myself well given the tremendous pressure I was under from the power-hungry opposition. But as anybody who has been in this business of international politics knows, the Tubabs are not that faithful to their friends. Their leaders are always taking the national pulse, organizing polls, taking decisions on the spur of the moment, and changing their minds to suit political exigencies of the moment. It would therefore be folly, even suicidal, for any African country to put their full trust and faith in them. History is replete with the littered corpses of Third World leaders whose only crime was that they loved the Tubabs too much.

The environment

The world is behaving today as if the environment has just been discovered. Yet it is as old as the hills.

People in Tubab are pointing to the forests in so-called Third World countries and saying all sorts of things about them. In the past it was obscene to have a jungle. Since they discovered that the jungle is rich in animals, medicinal plants, timber, minerals, etc., the same people who were desecrating it have now turned to worshipping it. We say we know hypocrisy when we see it.

All this is also happening because the Tubabs have realized that destruction of our forests and jungles can spell their own destruction. Yet they are the very people who, in the name of civilization and trade, started over-exploiting our forests.

As industries churn out millions of products daily, so too do they churn out tons upon tons of waste. Any wonder that the Tubabs are turning towards Third World countries to accept their waste materials for safekeeping? There is nothing devious or insidious about this. Don't they dump on us, in the name of food aid and trade, food that even their animals wouldn't eat?

Let me state in unmistakable terms my government's position on this burning issue of the environment.

Dumping of Waste

My government was accused by a few blighted souls of entering into a secret arrangement with a Tubab waste disposal company for millions of tons of waste to be dumped somewhere in Mandzah. These renegades of the truth went further to say that I accepted a paltry amount for the disposal, and planned to dump the waste in the part of the country where I am most unpopular.

I consider these accusations as a slur on my reputation that I have been trying to clean up over the past five years. Let the truth ring out that I never entered nor contemplated entering any secret pact with any individual, company or government for industrial waste to be dumped in my country.

The facts of the matter are that I was contacted by the wife of the friend of my son-in-law's brother who lives in Tubab to accept a few tons of scrap metal to be dumped in my country. At first I demurred, but when she said it would not be free, I then changed my mind and accepted it merrily. Obviously I couldn't have charged her too much as we were talking about scraps of metal and not waste. The charge that I asked for a paltry $5 a ton for the waste is therefore unfounded because I was charging for scrap metal and not for the metal works.

It is correct that we agreed that the best place to bury this scrap metal would be in the north of our country where there is little rainfall. We did not want the heavy torrential rains of the south to carry scraps of metal all over the country.

As to the charge that I chose the north because it is, as far as my government is concerned, enemy territory, I say nothing can be further from the truth. The lies that men tell shall live after them. My government does not have any enemies, nor do I consider any ethnic group in this country my enemies. I have lived a rich and full life in which I have dedicated myself wholeheartedly to forging national unity and peace in this country. Those who want to take the sword of calumny, slander and blackmail will meet in me a valiant match.

Let me now touch on another related subject. We in Mandzah don't need to be told how to run our affairs. Rumours have also been circulating that a Tubab company fooled us and instead of sending us fertilizer, it sent us industrial waste. I know the difference between fertilizer and industrial waste.

When the John Doe Chemicals Company in Tubab Twelve contacted Mr. Chifo, member of my delegation during my visit to Tubab Twelve last year, I remember very well that we spoke about fertilizer and not about industrial waste. It was understood, though we never specifically mentioned the type of fertilizer, that the company would be sending us something called fertilizer for our northern farmers.

Our enemies have passed word round that we had requested radioactive waste to bury in the north so as to debilitate, maim and kill the people from that region. I am trembling as I write this because such blatant lies were meant to drive a wedge between the northern people of my country and my government. That way our detractors would then turn round and tell the world that my own people hate me. Thank God our security people are vigilant and have not allowed any discontent to break out in the north of Mandzah.

It is indeed ironic that the voices that are being heard today championing Third World causes are the same that are muted when two African countries are wreaking havoc on each other.

All the arms and nerve gases that are used in fratricidal Third World Wars are not manufactured in Third World countries. The Third World is being used as the dumping ground for weapons and the test site for new destructive armaments. Yet the world is silent because it does not believe that its own survival is threatened. What does it matter to them if the Third World destroys itself as long as some of us will rise up from the ashes and sign lucrative contracts for their companies to rebuild our shattered cities, industries, economies, and way of life.

The government of the Republic of Mandzah believes that as long as we so-called Third World nations do not realize that all the wars we are fighting against one another are remote-controlled, we shall remain in submissive subordination because Tubabs believe that their economic survival depends on the political subversion of our people.

I shall make a disclosure today that I suspect may shock the world, but I feel compelled to do this now because I am cleansing my conscience and calling on my African brothers and sisters to understand some of the sinister ways in which we are being held hostage in our own countries.

About ten years ago, a former prime minister of Tubab Nine sent me a telex that he would like to meet me during a trip he had heard I would be making to his country. I responded that it would be a pleasure for me to see him again as I had lost contact with him since he left office. I considered him a friend and recall sending him a small amount, through his personal bank account, to help with his election campaign. These are things we leaders usually do because our own political fortunes depend to a large extent on how well we consolidate our relations with our Tubab friends and foreign backers. He lost the election, but that is another matter.

During the Tubab Nine trip, I received my friend in my castle in his country's capital. We chatted amiably, recalled some of the good times we had shared together, and promised to keep in closer touch. Before my friend left, he held my hand to shake it, but tarried awhile. He was about to say something but then he just as quickly swallowed it. I realized that he was not looking at me.

When he lifted his head, I saw that his eyes runneth over with tears. I felt embarrassed and asked him what was wrong. He took a deep breath, held my hand firmer and said he would confess something he learned one of his ministers had done to me while he was prime minister. He said he would not reveal the name of the minister because he had since become the chairman of the board of a company that was doing brisk business with my country.

Amidst sighs and with tears flowing down generously on his cheeks, he said one of his ministers had taken advantage of our friendship and had accepted a bribe from a company to dump waste in my country. He described the area in my country elaborately. I thanked him and said I would get back to him after making my own investigations.

At the end of my trip, I returned home and our investigations showed that the village where the chemical had reportedly been dumped produced the highest number of our mental patients, fools and idiots. They were worse than our political prisoners. In my precipitation, I had forgotten to ask the former prime minister about the name of the product.

I immediately dispatched my new minister of health, hospitalisation and death, Dr. Etsahmben, to see the former prime minister and report on what we had discovered. When Dr. Etsahmben arrived in the capital of Tubab Nine, he called my friend from his hotel room and took an appointment to meet him in a local restaurant. To our greatest dismay, the former prime minister never reached the restaurant. He was found murdered in his car. Dr. Etsahmben called his house after waiting for hours in vain, but the telephone had suddenly gone out of order. I have since then tried unsuccessfully to reach the man's family, and have not been able to obtain the police report on his death.

Public Works

In our drive to revive the ailing agricultural sector and ensure sustainable agricultural production, it is imperative that we rehabilitate all our farm-to-market roads and open up our farming communities to the modern world by providing adequate schools, dispensaries, markets, recreational facilities, etc.

After long drawn-out negotiations with the Tubab Solidarity Bank, the International Loan Shark Fund, the African Economic Union, and some private banks, we are proud to say that we have now obtained all the loans we applied for to construct some feeder roads and rehabilitate our major footpaths. The officials of the various loan institutions have already received their bribes and commissions, and have speeded up the processing of all the papers.

Now that the paper work is finished, we shall immediately launch the pre-feasibility study. Once that is done, there will be a pre-qualification call for tenders, short-listing of the qualified civil engineering companies, and an interview.

The minister of urban and rural destruction met with me yesterday to work out the amount of bribes the short-listed companies should be mandated to pay, and how the funds should be shared among key government officials and then transferred abroad to the various accounts. This, of course, is the most difficult decision in the whole process of selecting a suitable civil engineering firm because it means haggling over money. Since objectivity will be our watchword, we shall award the contract to the firm that is willing to pay the highest amount of bribes and commissions in advance.

Once the foreign banks have certified that the funds have been credited to our personal national accounts, we shall immediately set up a committee of some of our eminent architects to supervise the work. The minister of urban and rural destruction has already established a committee to screen applicants.

The committee will include, but not necessarily be restricted to, Joromi Ashia, doctor of block-making and bricklayer attached to the Muyengo mission hospital, Nyam Mbab Kana, chief draughtsman in the bureaucracy department of the ministry of public works, roads and gutters, Adolf Manpassman, Mandzah's gold medallist in the Mount Mandzah 10,000 meter race, and Shiri Wanwei Wanmamboh, Mandzah's only female architect and adviser to the President on slumps and squatter matters.

In undertaking the rehabilitation work, our architects must watch out because we have been disappointed in the past with the sloppy work done on our roads. Our country receives thousands of millimetres of rain every year, which washes off the tar with the result that the lifespan of our roads is never more than four years.

I am currently investigating unfounded allegations that the minister of urban and rural destruction is responsible for the rain and for the poor state of our roads.

Rain, we all know, comes from heaven. I really fail to see what the minister of URUD has to do with it. Nonetheless, to prove our detractors wrong, we shall establish a Presidential Rain Commission to study what we can do to ensure that we receive just the quantity of rain we want, and when we want it. Minister Fineboy Njumba has already proposed the names of the Rain Commission members. They are: Dr. Wankwa Ndongben, Mandzah's foremost witch doctor and rain maker; Rev. Fidelis Achu Firi, headmaster of the Remember the Deluge School; Dr. Innocent Mbon, lecturer in Botany at the National University and Mr. Gregg Thomas, Tubab expert and English Language instructor at the President Wan Nei National School of the Deaf and Dumb. The diversity of skills of members of the committee will certainly be an asset.

I do not wish to pre-empt the results of the work of the Rain Commission, but it has been said in many quarters that we are not building our roads well because the funds allocated for the project are being stolen by those handling the project. I have never heard anything so stupid. No one, as far as I know, has stolen any of the money. Misappropriating funds and stealing money are different things. While we are open to criticism, I think people should be constructive in the way they criticize the government.

A few unpatriotic journalists and their equally unpatriotic editor paymasters decided last year that because their newspapers were experiencing an unprecedented decline in sales, they would start peddling gossips and fabricated stories. They thought of no better name to blaspheme than that of my aunt.

My auntie, Princess Abu Frida Wanmanam, after whom the government and the party have named countless schools, bridges, highways, and public buildings in recognition of her role as the Mother of the Supreme Leader of Mandzah, ordered the minister of public works, roads and gutters to divert the highway passing near her home because, even though she had become deaf and blind through age, she couldn't stand the noise from passing cars nor the sight of the ghastly accidents that are always taking place below her home.

The minister immediately took action and an international civil engineering firm had to be hired overnight to divert the road. Luckily for the government, the minister had shares in the firm and so the work was completed in a record two months at slightly less than what it would normally have cost government if we had farmed out the work to some other firm.

The opposition papers made so much fuss about the highway diversion as if the government would go broke from such a small project. The funny thing about the entire mass media mass hysteria is that the funds weren't even ours. This is money that we borrowed after submitting an excellent request that the donors considered very favourably. The donors were so happy with the soundness of the project that they recommended we transfer the People's Lagoon from its present site to another part of town. Our experts are working with their experts on the project and, before long, we would be the first country in the world to have moved a lagoon from one part of town to another. Again, it wouldn't cost our people anything because we will be granted a loan to pay for it.

There are many other public works development projects in the pipeline. We hope that in the next five years, we will have a 246 kilometre two-lane highway linking our country's capital city with my farm, my golf course and hunting grounds. We have already been guaranteed the funds to build an international casino on the leeward side of Mount Mandzah that belongs to my family.

Culture

No people can claim to be a people if they do not have a culture. Culture, after all, is the distinguishing feature of any people. When the colonialists came to Africa, we were taught that we were backward and that we would remain forever so if we did not adopt western values and culture.

At independence, we were neither African nor Tubab, neither black nor white. We had been caught in the middle of opposing forces. While we cannot affirm that we have succeeded in getting rid of the colonialist's brainwashing, it is gratifying to note that all African countries today are proud of their blackness and are doing everything possible to impose black culture on a credulous world.

I am proud of my government's policy to revive our culture and give more meaning to our people's quest for originality. The minister of culture and imitation has produced what is the first blueprint of a cultural awareness program anywhere in Africa.

Those of our citizens who listen to our national radio and watch television will have realized that we are endeavouring to bring our culture to our people in the comfort of their homes. While government is bending backwards to stimulate interest in our culture, some foreigners and a few misguided nationals say we are not doing enough. They claim that showing a few breasts on television will not revive our culture, and that what we should be doing is targeting the urban areas where our so-called westernized populations live.

People must wake up to the enormity of the task of cultural revival. A people's culture has to do with their everyday life: their food, the way they eat, dress, pray, interact, behave, live, survive, die, etc. Government cannot possibly regulate all these aspects of its people's collective existence. What we have tried to do is draw the people's attention to some of our culture's vanishing acts.

We shall build more cultural centres throughout the length and breadth of this country to enable our youth, on whom the future of this country depends, to organize disco dance competitions and to watch the latest films from the Holy Woods and Phindia. There can be no better way of ensuring the cultural reawakening of our people.

At the same time, we shall continue to portray our culture in civic displays. The Cultural Revival Society has proposed the following measures within the framework of our Five Year Plan.

1. My government should strictly enforce a cultural code of conduct and behaviour. All citizens should therefore freely give up their colonial Christian names in favour of local names. To that end, government should establish a Name Committee to find local equivalents of biblical and historical names.
2. In view of the fact that we have been receiving fewer and fewer tourists and visitors, anthropologists, sociologists, historians and journalists in the last few years – very likely because they think we do not have anything original to show

them – government should rekindle their interest by imposing a national dress code. Thus, the official attire to all Mandzah official functions will be any animal skin. We expect ecologists to raise hell but we know how to handle them. As soon as Tubabs hear that there is a newly discovered race wearing nothing but animal skins, we stand to receive an endless stream of tourists.

Religion

Religion is one of most controversial issues in history. Wars have been fought over it, families divided because of it, and heads of state deposed because of it. My government believes that our people are mature enough to indulge in any religion that they think meets their aspiration for redemption and salvation.

Visitors to our country usually marvel at the religious tolerance and freedom our people and foreigners enjoy. They will bear witness and testimony to the fact that we have churches, mosques, synagogues, shrines, riverbanks, tree trunks and other places of worship for our people. And if they walk down our streets, they will see representatives of various churches, denominations, sects and cults canvassing for souls and fishing in the troubled waters of their community.

However, as much as my government believes in religious freedom, we think we must put some order in the myriads of religious groups that are springing up everyday. Soon the whole country will be overrun by religious groups and cults of all kinds that are taking up our best land and paying absolutely no taxes.

It is this government's policy not to interrupt people who have elected to dream, hallucinate or chant at will in the name of God. We most certainly do not intend to stifle the people's creative genius. We would rather want that creative genius to be channelled to solving the traditional problems that old-fashioned religion as we know it set out to correct.

As a government, we also believe that the church should preach God's Word that says, among other things, that Christians should give to God what is God's and to Caesar what is Caesar's. The church should not meddle in things that do not concern it. And if Christians want to speak in tongues, this government cannot prevent them. However, we believe we should remind our people that we have a national tongue.

As we see it, old-fashioned religion has lost its spark for, while the number of religious groups and cults is increasing everyday, so too is society degenerating steadily. One has the sneaky suspicion that there is some correlation between the two.

I myself was raised by missionaries who came to Africa with the Bible as their weapon to fight against what they saw as our pagan ways. But if what we see today is any guide, my government believes it is time for the so-called missionaries to fight against all the marks of paganism that we see in their own countries – worship of money instead of God, avarice, greed, racism, lust for power, rampant fornication, disrespect for one's elders, adultery etc. I challenge any God-fearing missionary to tell me in all sincerity whether more sins are being committed in Tubab or in Africa.

I say we in Africa have been fooled for too long. The missionaries are out to do for us what they cannot do for their own people. There is no reason why they should pretend to love us more than they do their own people who are crying out there in the cold wilderness of despair and despondency for help. One has the feeling that Tubab missionaries have given up on their own people, but we say they can still be saved. They need to be rescued from the cults.

We in Africa believe that evangelization must begin in Tubab and that, given the pervasive influence of Tubab's lack of culture on the rest of the world, the church should reinforce its activities throughout Tubab. We in Africa are living in peaceful co-existence with our gods.

Sports

One area in which the black man has left footprints on the sands of time is sports. I remember quite vividly the message Jesse Owens sent to Hitler and his mythical Aryan race when he won four gold medals in the 1936 Olympic Games in Berlin.

My government has been informed that some Tubab research scientists plan to use black people in an experiment to produce white athletic clones in a bid to reform athletics and correct the present distortions that favour the black man. We further understand that this plan is part of an overall strategy to produce a new breed of sportsmen generally.

Hitler, recent events show us, may have passed away, but not his ideas. Is the world not witness to a new breed of messengers of evil that are waging an innovative, racist, dehumanising and barbaric struggle against blacks and other groups the world over?

While deploring all these actions in the strongest possible terms, it is a sad reflection on human cynicism that had these champions of hate not also cast the spell of racism on some white groups, the world might not have stirred, still. In other words, had they restricted their smear campaign to blacks, no one would have bothered. Until we realize that the humiliation of one race is the humiliation of mankind as a whole, we shall know no peace.

In the light of the increasing popularity of sports all over the world, my government has decided to use sports as a balm to heal ethnic wounds and to foster harmonious relations and thus distract the people's attention from economic, social and political problems at home.

All African countries today recognize the potent force of sports as a political weapon. We are therefore in good company in making sports development our second national priority after defence. Our sportsmen and women are our accredited ambassadors. Take, for example, our performance in the Universal Dope Sports Meet that takes place every four years. It is generally recognized that we are usually beaten because we refuse to listen to the advice of the national coach we sent to spy on the Tubabs.

Our national coach, Mr. Atam Tseboh, had counselled massive doping, but I overruled him. I now realize that we politicians and political leaders must give full rein to our technical staff to take technical decisions. Had we doped like our adversaries, I am sure we would have won lots of medals.

That experience has taught us that we should not allow doping in future sports' meets to be the exclusive preserve of a particular group of people. Either we take part fully in the Dope Meet by accepting to dope ourselves very high or we organize our own low-level Dope Sports Meet. But it is only fair, we believe, that the Dope Sports Federation should come out with guidelines as to the amount of dope that each athlete is supposed to have in his or her blood. We don't want to be penalized for not having any dope in our blood.

Furthermore, I have announced to the nation that as far as the other forms of sport are concerned, my country will not relent in lending them our full backing and support. Accordingly, our Sports Council has, on the recommendation of the Botoh Committee established by the Presidential Sports Reform Commission, made a number of proposals that I fully endorse. We are convinced that if these proposals are fully implemented, they will harness the full sports potential in this country and stimulate sports development as a whole in the next decade.

Football

I am aware that there is widespread discontent about the performance of our national football team in spite of the fact that I have staked both my personal fortune and prestige to ensuring victory for the team. Yet the boys continue to play as if lead is tied to their feet.

I don't believe there's any president anywhere in the world that allows one of his private planes to be used as a taxi, carrying players up and down the world whenever there is an international match. This I do because I love my country. One would have expected that these sacrifices I am making out of love for my country will pay off and that our people will see my good works and glorify my name. Instead of lavish praise for me, some unpatriotic individuals are accusing me of giving too much importance to football and neglecting the other areas of underdevelopment.

I have always said that when people do not know anything, they should not be ashamed to ask. It is surprising that some citizens have not fully grasped the essence of our sports policy. All they have to do is look at the world around them. Woe betide a country that does not take football seriously.

In the light of this situation, I have adopted our football players as my children. Yet, whenever they have problems, instead of coming to see me, they run to the press and tell the world that they are not being taken care of; that unless I recruit a foreign coach they are not going to win a match; that I should pass a decree banning people from considering footballers as school dropouts and tramps, etc.

I have heard these complaints before, and have appealed to my boys that if they want to dispel the negative things people are saying about them, they should let their light shine before men so that they may see their good works and glorify them. They should bring home victory and prove the sceptics wrong since victory is the essence of sports.

Some people say sports should be practised for sports' sake. I say that's bunk. The length to which nations are going today to develop sports shows to what length the world will go to test the limits of human endurance and strength. Sports has become more than entertainment since national honour is at stake.

In response to our national football team's continued lacklustre performance, we decided to enlist all the players in the armed forces in the hope that discipline would be instilled into them and thus guarantee victory. How wrong we were. Not only did they turn out to be sloppy marksmen, but they couldn't score a goal. Then the other enlisted men became jealous because of the preferential treatment we were giving the football players.

However, not being one to be easily discouraged by a few disappointing results, I decided to give the team another chance. We gave each of the players a villa, a car and a scholarship after the team drew with the Praying Mantis of Njingyi and the Locusts of Njinmambang. That was two years ago, and since then the team has lost all its matches. We had hoped that it would bring home at least one trophy. We decided to kick the players out of the villas, disband the team, and recruit new players.

We have great faith in the new crop of young players. We are sure that money will not be their greatest consideration, and that they will be playing to defend their national colours. We must revive the old spirit of nationalism, patriotism, and dedication to the cause of one's country.

I invite the youth of this country to take their cue from me, my ministers, and party militants. At the last meeting of the African Sports Ministers Council, I am told that the meeting focused on the ways and means of thwarting our young men's insatiable lust for money. Our youth no longer consider playing at home as a national assignment. They easily succumb to the lure of money because international sports have become a moneymaking venture. What a shame that chivalry has lost its shine in sports.

Let me now discuss another subject that has been pending for quite some time. Last year a foreign journalist asked me to shed light on the rumour surrounding Deuteronomy Abakwa, the most sensational Mandzah footballer of all time, who was found murdered in his girlfriend's house two years ago. At the time, I said my government was still investigating the crime and that I would disclose the results of the police investigations to the world.

I believe my autobiography is an appropriate medium to tell the world what I know really happened following a very meticulous investigation by our security people.

Abakwa was known throughout the world as Mandzah's foremost sportsman. After playing in Mandzah for the two leading clubs, The Mandzah White Devils and later on the Ndongben Poisoned Arrows, he signed a very lucrative six-figure contract with the Eleven Goal Merchants Football Club in Tubab Five. While playing for the Goal Merchants, he returned home from time to time to play for our national side whenever we had an international match. He was very popular and his name became a household word in Mandzah. One day I called Abakwa to my office, and under the glare of television lights, I publicly thanked him for the services he was rendering our country. I said all Mandzahs were proud of him because he had put us on the world football map and that he should devote his energies to his club and country. I then bestowed on him Mandzah's greatest honour, the President Wan Nei Medal of Valour, named after me.

I was surprised when, a few weeks after that, I heard that Abakwa had joined a roving gang of traitors to betray their country by criticizing me, the party, and government. I sent emissaries to find out the truth because I did not believe that an intelligent fellow like Abakwa would be so stupid as not to see my good works and glorify my name. Besides, I had taken Abakwa into confidence and made him my special assistant and roving ambassador.

What my people found out was that Abakwa now considered that because he was a football superstar and was known all over the world, he was untouchable and could go round saying all sorts of damaging things about his country. This is a boy to whom

I had given a villa and many other gifts.

I cannot forget when Abakwa lost his father. Even though the old man had never been a civil servant, government was responsible for the burial and all funeral expenses. I did this because Abakwa was a hero in his own way.

When I sent for Abakwa to find out the truth from him about the rumours I had heard, he reportedly told my minister of state security, spying and coups that he was more popular than I, and that it was just a matter of time before he would be sitting in my seat. He said he did not see how, he who was now rubbing shoulders with Tubab leaders and millionaires, could come and see me. He said if I wanted to see him, I should take an appointment with his public relations officer.

When you hear a thing like that, your first immediate reaction is to say it is not possible. My own immediate reaction was that money had probably deranged the poor little boy, or as they say, genius always carries with it the germ of abnormality.

On the strength of all the information we had gathered, we decided that Abakwa must be brought home to explain his conduct. Bringing him home was no big deal. One of our many female security officers who was a fake student in Tubab Five organized a party to which Abakwa and some of his cohorts were invited. The girls got Abakwa into his normal state of drunkenness and, with the help of a Tubab doctor, he was made to sleep sound enough for the duration of their flight here. We had to be careful not to arouse suspicion because his club would have made a lot of noise. We forged a letter in his handwriting and sent it to the club to say Abakwa was rushing home for the weekend to attend to some pressing family business.

It is a sordid lie that my security people killed Abakwa. We think he was the victim of internal feuding between factions of his so-called Grassroots Revolutionary Army. We have so far been unable to establish how he even got to his girlfriend's house. This murder or suicide is baffling to us just as it is to the rest of the world. We in this government, as everyone knows, do not approve murders of this kind. When we have to routinely eliminate someone, we do a clean job and don't leave a smoking gun.

Our security forces are on the lookout for leads, and whenever there is a breakthrough in the case, we shall, as we always have done, inform the world. Two years is a relatively short time in crime detection, and we are certain that no matter how long it takes, we shall someday unravel the mystery surrounding Abakwa's death.

Athletics

It is disgraceful that with all the hills, mountains and forests in Mandzah, we have been unable to train our athletes to win international athletic competitions. Small countries such as Ndom, Mbab, Dzoh and Angenge have made beating us their national pastime. In fact, there is indeed no genuine reason why we too should not be winning medals in athletic competitions. Aren't we too black?

In any case, I do not agree with those who say that the conveniences of modern life are affecting our people's stamina. When Jesse Owens won the four Olympic Gold Medals in 1936, he was, of all colours, black, running against the Aryans. And don't anyone tell me he had any modern conveniences. I believe, if I am not mistaken, he was then still a slave.

Other forms of sports

After football and athletics, we shall develop the other forms of sports as funds become available. This government's commitment to the development of sports is firm and rooted in my belief that all work and no play makes Jack a poor and dull little thing.

During my recent trip to Tubab, I was taken to a sports arena where I saw charming damsels gliding gracefully and majestically on ice. I was also taken uphill in the heart of the snow season and shown people running downhill on what looked liked crutches. How people on crutches can be running downhill at that speed I cannot understand. They say that sport is called skiing. I must say I fell for both the skating and the skiing.

After I returned home, I proposed to the minister of youths and sports to develop skating and skiing in Mandzah. He explained that we needed snow and ice but that should be no problem. I have already signed a bilateral sports agreement with Tubab Twenty to supply us with the snow and ice. I understand their snow and ice manufacturers are ecstatic about the possibility of opening up a new market for these two products. The snowploughs they sold to us last year as tractors will come in handy.

In conclusion, let me say that although we might not have won medals on the field of play in international sports competitions, it doesn't really matter. Since no one expected us to win, not even ourselves, no one was surprised. But that is not what got me mad.

During the opening ceremony of the recent Alambic Games, I was as mad as hell to see that no one was clapping for our delegation even though my government had spent quite a lot of money on the best designer suits. The crowd was instead cheering for delegations that wore national costumes and even for those that went to the extent of wearing animal skins. We thought we were dealing with civilized society and that we had to show our colonial parents that we have civilized taste.

Another thing struck me. We were going to compete in just four events as I had been made to understand. But I almost fell off my rocking chair when I saw on television that our delegation was made up of six athletes and 15 officials. To make matters worse, the head of the delegation was my minister of youth and sports himself. His wife, sister-in-law, uncle, grandmother and five of their eleven children were in the crowd waving to him as the delegation marched round the stadium triumphantly. They had flown at government's expense to attend the games.

When the delegation returned, the press announced jubilantly that I would fire the minister. When I transferred him from the ministry of youth and sports to trade and industry, the mass media launched a smear campaign against the minister and I for nothing.

9

The Debt Problem

The debt problem is one of mankind's greatest afflictions. It is a common, benign disease that initially affected the developed world primarily. However, when it started being transmitted to the Third World, it became very fatal. Its agents of transmission are the International Loan Shark Fund and the International Lenders Association. The Third World has been pleading unsuccessfully for the developed world to help find a cure for debt but they will not listen because while it affects them, somewhat, it does not kill them. Apparently it has been programmed to kill only Third World countries.

Surprisingly, quite a lot is known about this deadly disease, but it is not in the interest of the developed world to find a cure for it because the more the Third World is indebted, that is, the more the Third world is afflicted by the debt virus, the weaker is its financial organism and the less immune it is to blackmail and dependence.

Money, we all know, is the sinews of development. The more indebted a country, the lesser is its scope for development. My country has categorically refused to pawn its development to a group of international swindlers – international shylocks – who are demanding a pound of flesh for a meagre loan that we contracted a few years ago.

One of my main regrets is that at independence, we refused on the grounds of financial propriety, to accept all the loans that were proposed to us. I now realize that it was a tactical mistake. We should have accepted them because experience has shown that to him who incureth many loans, more money shall be given.

The world probably is not aware of the tremendous pressure that some international financial institutions bring to bear on us because they want us to accept their money. They say money is meant to float round and not to sit idly in banks. In most cases, I respond quite honestly that I do not need their money because I have already amassed enough, but they will not listen. International financial institutions are really hard of hearing.

Usually, because of their insistence and persistence, most African leaders quite grudgingly contract the debt virus. In some cases, this means mortgaging the future development of their countries because of cutthroat interest rates. When you tell the international financial institutions quite frankly that money does not mean much to you because you already have more than you need, they simply feign ignorance and pretend that they don't understand your tribal language.

In any case, before we realize it, the international network of money people has sent experts – those ubiquitous consultants whose avowed aim is to damage first and then repair later – to convince you that you need the money whether or not you need it and whether or not you can pay back. When at long last they have whetted your appetite enough and seen that you now need the money you do not need, they then lay down a series of humiliating conditions that you must accept.

My country is currently going through the humiliating exercise of debt negotiations. We have been called all sorts of names because we are unable to cough up the money that was forcibly shoved down our throats. I have maintained that we cannot pay back the money, especially as the interest alone has more than doubled the capital. They are now begging me to take another loan to pay the interest on the first loan so that I will have a clean record to show that I did not default on the first loan so that I can be eligible for another loan

Of course, I am being put up to public ridicule. The whole world is now prying into my personal life and wealth. Pressure is being brought to bear on me from all quarters to sell some of my private planes and castles in Tubab and so on. My government asserts that this is most unfair and unjust, especially as our Tubab negotiators knew all along that I did not want the money and that, having decided to take it, I was going to buy the two planes and build castles in the air. Now I cannot walk around in peace either in my country or abroad because wherever I go, I am welcomed with placards saying I am a thief.

I have advised the international financial community to look at the other countries that are more riddled with debt than we are, but they respond cynically that a debt-riddled body looks more attractive than one without debt wounds on it. The debt-riddled countries thus continue to receive a steady stream of financial doctors to tell them what to do to contract more debt.

We agree that debt is fatal, but blackmail is more fatal. Early this month, a delegation from the International Lenders Association (ILA) came to my country to teach us how to restructure our economy so as to put it on a sounder footing and thus enable us to contract more debt. We say we want more money, not more debt; we want more help, not more aid.

If my recollection is correct, there was a lot of talk last year about the use to which I had put loan money. In fact, there was even widespread speculation as to the full amount we had received and as to what had happened when the ILA announced that it was going to suspend further aid to my country because we had ostensibly failed to account for the money loaned to us.

Let me set out by first explaining that I and I alone decide how national funds have to be disbursed. I took this position after several persons in whom I had infinite trust disappointed me. Trusted companions to whom I remitted money to take abroad to my personal national bank account disappeared into thin air with the money. In other cases, some of them simply embezzled the funds, built mansions for themselves and their mistresses, and lived in the lap of luxury while the people for whom they were supposed to be toiling wallowed and languished in abject poverty.

My office oversees all state funds. To do this effectively, we have opened several bank accounts. I do not think it would be wise to reveal the account numbers or the banks in which the accounts are held because some street-smart government officials might hatch a plot, imitate my signature, and rob the state of all its funds. My son did that last year and squirreled away a couple of million dollars.

As to the use to which the funds are put, I believe the people and the world need to know how our hard-earned money is spent. I shall deal with this later.

International economists are the first people to say that the more money we make, the more money will be taken away from us. And our creditors continue to insist that I lay off civil servants, give more incentives to the private sector, and shore up our national currency, the Kapa. I am not sure these experts understand the workings of our African economies.

First of all, it is out of order to ask a President like me who loves his country to dismiss people from their jobs for no reason. I have to love my country because if I wasn't President of Mandzah, I don't see which other country would have accepted someone like me to be its President.

I am not sure these experts realize that most of the key civil servants in Mandzah come from my ethnic group and that they have a divine right to lead our civil service and execute the government's will. The suggestion would therefore have made sense some years ago before the ill-fated coup attempt led by Captain Chop Koki.

Prior to the coup attempt, I believed firmly that I could trust all ethnic groups in my country, but Chop Koki and his hired killers proved to me that people from the Mahbit tribe hate my people. I have since then fired all of them from government for their part in the coup attempt, thus leaving the country in the hands of people from my ethnic group.

Second, I agree with donors' suggestion that I should not recruit more civil servants for the time being. Since mass unemployment is the policy advocated by the ILA – which, by the way, is also our stated policy – we will hold the line on employment.

Third, the suggestion that I should give more incentives to the private sector is in line with what we have been doing since independence. Our economy is in the hands of foreigners because we have given them all the incentives they need to compete favourably with our own people, especially in key sectors of the economy such as agriculture, trade, money doubling, and transportation that require highly technical skills that our people do not possess. The results of our far-reaching policies are there for anyone to see.

A visitor to our country who goes to any of our markets will see that we have businessmen from all parts of the world. I do not know of any country in the world that has given foreigners as much legal protection as we have to exploit our country at will.

I take the same approach in my government. We have given adequate incentives to technical experts, consultants, advisers, foreign trade delegations, foreign businessmen and tourist to accept potions in our government and industry. For example, the entire security force guarding me and strategic areas of Mandzah comes from the Romance Republic, the Promised Republic, the United Conquerors Republic, the Hegemony Republic, etc. There are many free-enterprise mercenaries and governments ready to provide us with their military know-how.

Anyone who thinks he can stage a coup against me and succeed must connive with them because a coup that doesn't have their blessing will not succeed. But then since I have made them shareholders and stakeholders in our country – against our people's will – they know that if I am overthrown, they stand to lose all the opportunities I have given them in my country.

In the area of agricultural development, the large plantations and smallholder farms have been in the hands of our foreign friends and neighbours since colonial times. The money they repatriate every year from our buoyant economy helps to bolster their country's sagging economy. It is hoped that as the economies of our foreign friends and neighbours become more buoyant, they too will, out of African solidarity, help to shore up our own steadily sagging economy. We must live up to the noble credo of African solidarity that we have been preaching.

Trade has been especially liberalized and most of the businessmen, market women and traders that control our economy are from other countries. Since our people prefer to spend their time buying anything that comes their way, we have given incentives to foreign traders to import all the luxury goods that our people like to buy, including food crops which we could produce in abundance but which, because of our reliance on the outside world to feed us, have been abandoned. I am referring to such nutritious food crops as our local rice, beans, millet, yams, plantains, etc.

I marvel at our fast pace of development when I sit in my lofty office and behold luxury cars of all makes gliding down our sleek streets as they manoeuvre to avoid potholes. This is a measure of our development, and we believe that this government deserves a pat on the back for accomplishing so much in so short a time. It has taken my other colleagues much longer to ruin their economies.

As far as money doubling is concerned, this is a very lucrative business in which most of us are involved. In order for the government to reap the benefits of money doubling, I made the state a majority partner in the National Money Doubling Bureau (NMDB) or, what is called in most counties, the mint. When the government needs money, it requests the NMDB to print it.

We have also entered into a cooperative relationship with some black market dealers to buy and sell foreign exchange. We provide them the capital to do this because we believe that it is better for government to regulate how the black market should perform.

As for transportation, it is our view that there can be no progress without a viable transport system. Since our nationals are afraid of taking the risks involved in the transportation business unless government constructs better roads, our foreign friends have agreed to come to our rescue. The only condition they have imposed is that our government should waive compulsory insurance cover on their vehicles and arraignment in the event of a traffic accident. It is our view that they are not asking for too much since none of us wishes an accident to take place. An accident is an accident.

Our policemen and customs officers have consequently been given strict orders to facilitate the transportation business of our foreign friends by restricting their demands for bribes to our people. Our foreign friends usually say they know more about contributing to campaign and slush funds than about giving bribes to our police officers. However, since they learn and adapt very fast, we should be more indulgent. There are enough bribes to go round and we do not have to behave as if I haven't deregulated bribery, patronage and corruption.

I would like to take this opportunity to re-state quite categorically that it is not the intention of my government to abolish bribery that we all know is an inexhaustible source of supplementary income for members of the cabinet, our people in uniform and civil servants.

As anyone who has been to Mandzah can readily testify, these key policies have been very successful. Our roads are paved with evil intentions and littered with the corpses of victims of road accidents. Government is doing everything possible to ensure that the roads are maintained in a permanent state of disrepair, and that road users pay increasingly more bribes. After all, accidents and corruption are some of the benefits of development, and we should be prepared to pay this as the price for moving in the fast lane.

10

Taxation

It is an error to believe that we make lots of money from taxes. Our people, taking their cue from those in government, have sharpened their ingenuity for tax evasion. The big guns are not paying the state a farthing. They own the big companies, the best homes, and choice land, and use their positions of influence to threaten the tax collectors. The result is that taxes are paid by the wretched of our earth that do not have the money to pay.

According to reports, our rich nationals have been imitating their tax-cheat brethren in other lands by writing off the expenses incurred for their face, tummy and fanny lifts, girlfriends, boobs, drugs, hookers, vacations, etc. as professional fees.

Whatever little tax money is collected is spent on the many underdevelopment projects that I have been undertaking since I became President of Mandzah. The money, of course, is too small to go round, and so there are disparities of income and in standards of living.

Tax money, for those who do not know, is my prime source of revenue. Our annual budget is based on expectations from tax collection, customs duty, etc. Until we were hard hit by the economic recession a few years ago, taxes generated much money.

I would like to mention some of the many development project undertaken with our valiant taxpayers money:

1. The People's House. It is a sprawling and sumptuous palace with a moat, a golf course, an artificial lake, a zoo, a park, a car-racing course for my children, and an airfield. We wanted something befitting of a Life-President. People who think this is expensive should visit the Holy Woods and Everly Hills in the United Conquerors Republic where most Tubab stars live.

2. Presidential Lodges around the country, complete with servants, cooks, guards, a detachment of the police and military force.
3. 4 jumbo jets and several helicopters in the presidential fleet.
4. 3 castles in Tubab.
5. Majority shares in the following companies: Mandzah Ocean Liners, Inc., Air Mandzah, Mandzah Transport Inc., Family Oil and Gas Corporation, Manufacturers' and Distributors Ltd., United Distillers, Mandzah Tobacco Company, Mandzah Hotels and Catering Corp., Mandzah Estates Development Corp., and Mandzah Mining, Fishing, Farming and Construction Company.
6. The 2,000 acre piece of land adjacent to the Shumbo Enen Island which I bought from the State 8 years ago. Most of the fish on our market comes from my island.

Our Five Year Plan calls for the acquisition by government of more public and private land for underdevelopment purposes.

Customs duty

I have already pointed out that one of the greatest sources of my revenue is customs duty. We need all the money we can collect to be able to fuel our economic recovery and to break the recession hammerlock on our economy.

Unfortunately for our country, our revenue hunters are getting richer and richer while the state gets poorer and poorer. I have dossiers piled up in my office of privileged groups that have obtained duty free privileges. While acknowledging that some key sectors of industry need a break (such as religious organizations, international agencies, embassies, the party, government, etc.), I fail to understand why intelligent people who are supposed to know better continue to file past my office expecting a waiver of customs duty.

From now on, government has decided to restrict the number of those entitled to duty free privileges. The list will appear in the Government Gazette, but suffice it for me to mention that in addition to those already enjoying the privilege, it has been extended to all foreign businessmen, experts, consultants, technical advisers, and senior government officials. We regret that we cannot extend it to everybody.

11

Internal Security

There is no nation in the world nor political party that allows its institutions to be transgressed at will. Governments, be they democratic as we are, autocratic, fascist, communist or socialist, maintain a vigilant security force that oversees the internal and international security of the state. In general, they spy on their enemies and try to neutralize them before they become effective, help friendly countries to ensue their stability, and maintain peace and stability at home.

We have sacred values that must be defended at all cost, and my government has made the guarantee of state security one of its foremost objectives. In order to do this, we have borrowed liberally from the way the security systems of other countries operate, adapted their systems to suit our purpose and, where necessary, innovated.

I have studied the security networks of other countries and can say quite convincingly that ours pales in their shadow. We do not have the elaborate networks that they have nor have we adapted their brutality. We in Mandzah believe that our people should be free to go about their daily business without fear of molestation.

Maybe it is because we have been tolerant of dissenting voices in our country that some people have taken that to mean weakness. Over the past 30 years, my government has been the target of evil forces bent on disuniting my people and diverting our attention from the task of nation building. I say enough is enough. Before I give the measures that the Mandzah Security Commission adopted some time ago, I shall first, for the record, go as far back as possible and describe the signposts on my country's security highway.

1962 Invasion

Barely two years after we achieved our independence, my director of security at the time, the late Nehemiah Mafe, discovered a plot being hatched by elements of the disgruntled and disbanded MIP to overthrow the freely elected government of the MAPU that I headed.

I, in my characteristic God-fearing manner, said I did not believe that Akwankwan Sobom, my disgraced minister of the armed forces who had been sacked for trying to create his own elite protection force, would contemplate not only overthrowing me but imposing a foreign ideology on our people. Little did I know the extent to which the human mind can go to contrive hate and treason.

Still naïve, I refused to take action to nip the plans in the bud. We decided to spy on a number of Sobom's close associates. It was not long before my security forces, in a routine road check, arrested Bih Muyen Azaah, secretary in the ministry of posts and telecommunications and a girlfriend of Sobom's former driver. She was carrying a bundle of money wrapped in the loincloth she had round her waist. When she was fully searched, the security people found a map of the national armoury in her possession.

The lady was whisked off to the Tisong state security office for interrogation. At first she refused to cooperate but when my people used some of the modern investigative methods they learned abroad, such as beatings, electrocution, starvation and torture, she admitted that the money had been given to her by one Malam Magida, a well known witch doctor who had been hired to ensure the success of the planned invasion.

Armed with this evidence, we set out to arrest the Malam and all those associated with him in one way or the other. Magida refused to cooperate and denied any involvement in an attempt to overthrow my government. He even denied any knowledge of Muyen Azaah and said he did not know Akwankwan Sobom.

The more Magida pleaded his innocence, the more he wrapped himself in the web of lies he was weaving. More damaging was the fact that Magida, through his persistent refusal to acknowledge that he knew Sobom, was implying that all my attempts to give a sound political education to my people had failed for it meant that the party militants had not been carrying out their indoctrination work well. I considered this an even more damaging revelation.

My security people were asked to arrest all those so-called party militants responsible for political indoctrination of the people. They had not been doing their work properly. There was a nationwide swoop on all villages, towns and cities. Thousands of people were arrested and locked up for questioning.

We did not want to take the law in our hands since the law must take its course. A number of military tribunals were hurriedly set up to try all those accused of not knowing Akwankwan Sobom because it showed that they were not interested in the political life of their country. As for those so-called militants responsible for indoctrination lessons, it was not necessary to try them since they were already guilty of wasting our country's meagre resources in the sense that they were being paid for work they were not doing.

While all this was going on, the Sobom group panicked, and seeing that their mischievous plan was going to fail, launched an armed attack on our people in the south. They had crossed into our country from Fuchiwe, and we had proof that they had received both military and financial help from the oppressive, corrupt and degenerate government of the unpopular, fledgling and tyrannical regime of Kwako Kwabog.

I want to pause here and pay tribute to those of our comrades in arms who lost their lives in battle to save the soul of our nation, and the spirit of the party. But for their selfless attachment to our cause, and the sacrifice of their lives in the defence of our democratic ideals, this nation that I have forged from the throes of disunity, tribalism, nepotism and war would once again have been the theatre of untold suffering, wanton death and chronic instability.

What haven't those who thrive on conspiracy said about us? That I am vain glorious, that I am a bloodthirsty hound, that I invent invasions and coups to get rid of my enemies, that I suppress the press, and so many other devilish things. I say if I am still in power today, it is by the will of the people for no one can do all the things I am accused of doing and not incur the wrath of the people.

Following the invasion, my people took the offensive. The armed forces and the whole country appealed to me to teach the traitors a lesson so as to dissuade those who, barren of constructive ideas, may want to endanger the future of our country through blind and selfish opportunism. For one entire week all work in Mandzah ground to a halt because the people, spontaneously and in unison, decided to organize solidarity rallies throughout the country to show the world out there that they love me, the party and its policies.

I resisted all attempts to execute the invaders, and even became a little unpopular with my own people as a result. But then I accepted a little unpopularity as the prize to pay for loving my people and my country. In other words, I turned the other cheek against the reasoned advice and counsel of the entire country.

My security people were specifically instructed not to do bodily harm to any of the ringleaders. We did not want to fight terror with terror for our people had known too much suffering and had paid a very heavy price for their independence.

All told, we arrested 123 invaders, killed more than 476 on the field of battle, and arrested 6109 of their collaborators. They who had sworn through leaflets and tracts to fight to the last man abandoned the fight when the tide of vengeance was against them.

That invasion was our nation's period of infamy. We contacted President Kwako Kwabog in neighbouring Fuchiwe to extradite those who had betrayed their country to face trial but Kwabog denied ever supporting and arming the ragtag and ramshackle band of traitors. By refusing to cooperate, Kwabog had transgressed one of the cardinal principles on which our fragile microstates were built, namely the principle of the sanctity of colonial borders. In arming the invaders, Kwabog had hoped to cause discontent so that members of the Katakata tribe my enemies claimed my government was maltreating would rise up against me.

In keeping with our obedience to God's command, and our respect for human life, we raised the issue of the invasion of our country at the meeting of the African Solidarity Union. We soon realized that it was a taboo subject and that no leader was prepared to discuss it.

I believe history will want to know exactly what happened to the kingpins of the invasion and all the detainees. As I have said, my government at the time took the decision that none of the ringleaders should be executed. We felt that they deserved a penalty was than death. History has a record of the crude barbarism wrought by man to man and we did not think we had the fertile imagination to surpass it.

As I look back to that period, I cannot help wondering why the world overreacted the way it did. My government received emissaries from different countries pleading with us to spare the lives of the traitors and asking for a fair trial for the murderers. That is the way of the world. The victim is always expected to show compassion and turn the other cheek.

The world should recall that two years ago when I celebrated the anniversary of my ascension to the throne of Life-President of Mandzah, I freed most of those rebels. The brain and mastermind of the carnage of his own people, Akwankwan Sobom, is back in his home village, blind, after Amnesia International intervened.

Beatrice Beriberi, the whore the murderers sent to scour the country, remains as unrepentant as ever, claiming that she had been framed and that she had never been involved in the invasion. True to her nature, she had twins in the tunnel with one of her guards and committed a series of abortions. I hope no one will say anymore that we deprived the prisoners of fun.

The list of those freed was read out on radio and television, and I invite the public and the foreign vociferous press to visit and interview them.

12

Plots

Following the numerous forms of treachery of which I, my government, party and country have been victims, we decided to institute a number of measures to ensure that traitors must be brought to book and made to face the wrath of the people they betray. No nation can be governed properly if traitors are allowed to walk about freely dispensing lies, defaming institutions and taking the law into their hands.

Accordingly, we have identified key groups in our society whose activities must be monitored on a permanent basis. Every country does that, and I believe if we had done this a long time ago, we would not have found ourselves in the mess in which we are today.

Espionage in politics and international affairs is an accepted way of life. In all my discussions with leaders of different political and economic persuasions, I have yet to meet a leader who does not swear by the name of his security chief.

One cannot talk about security without talking about espionage. The Tubabs, from whom cometh the church and political doctrines of all kinds, have refined espionage and raised it to a pure art form. In a nutshell, espionage for them has become an industry. They are forever seeing real and imagined enemies against whom they must manufacture the most sophisticated espionage gear.

My government has had its own generous share of espionage activities. In order to cover the tracts of those who responded to this national calling, I am sure the reader will forgive me if I do not call names.

Our espionage activities are still targeted to the following unruly groups (not necessarily in order of intelligence): politicians, security forces, party militants, students, government officials, embassies, civil servants, traditional rulers and the general population. Unlike other African countries, however, we do not believe in subjugating our people to the tyranny of constant espionage.

The Armed Forces

It is well known that we spend at least 50% of our annual budget on the armed forces. We think this is normal given the constant threat we face from our enemies both from within and outside the country. After everything is considered, given the pivotal role our people's army is playing in the life of the nation, I believe it makes a lot of sense to increase their budget.

A delegation from all branches of the armed forces came to see me a few months ago and, pointing a gun to my head, made me sign that their budget will be increased by a meagre 10% next year. I find this slight increase very reasonable in the face of the galloping inflation that is undermining our economic efforts.

The armed forces, as everyone knows, constitute the lifeblood of any nation. The integrity and security of the state depend on them as the last bastion of our collective existence as a people and a nation.

There have been comments from many quarters about the arrogance, brutality and inefficiency of our armed forces. Anyone who insults our subservient army of valiant men and women in arms is insulting me because I owe my long reign to them.

The world's memory, regrettably, is very short. Today the army is the envy of everyone when, during colonial times and at independence, only people from my ethnic group were willing to risk joining it since we were considered illiterate and not good enough to serve in the civil service. However, since the army started wielding tremendous political power to the point of destabilizing democracy, intellectuals are now flocking to us to recruit them. Where were they when my village and tribal boys were defending our country?

Our army has fought some tough historic battles to maintain the integrity of our country. Two years ago it smashed the student rebellion on the university campus, crushed the incipient insurrection by market women nine months ago, arrested all the trade union leaders for organizing a peaceful demonstration to call government's attention to flaws in the Labour Code, effectively manned all polling stations in the last presidential election to ensure that all ballot boxes were carefully stuffed, brutalized our people for supporting the opposition rallies, etc. In the light of such sparkling victories, it is normal that our armed forces should be proud.

Recently, in the wake of the so-called revival of the democratic movement in Mandzah, our army has once again been championing the defence of our national institutions. A few opposition diehards have been trying, with the support of outside forces, to overthrow my government by a diabolical democratic method called elections. I thank God that we have Generals in our army who care about this country and who refuse to be used by politicians for their own selfish purposes.

While the armed forces as a whole have sworn to uphold the principles enshrined in our sacred constitution, some of the enlisted men and women have sought to use their uniforms as passports to power. We remember only too well the bloody disturbances that took place some years ago between various factions of the armed forces.

As commander-in-chief of the armed forces of this country, I am gratified to say that I have received the full cooperation of each branch of our armed forces: the army, air force, navy, police, gendarmerie, the presidential guards, the special paratroopers, the elite commando, etc.

In order to avoid the petty jealousies that usually tear apart such disparate self-seeking groups, I decided, in my capacity as guardian of the constitution, to make each branch of the armed forces autonomous from the other.

I have further been taxed of lavishing gifts and money on our armed forces to cow them. This is an insult to them and me because they are professional people who think very highly of money and power. I have given strict orders that since our armed forces are the guardians of our country's security, the minister of finance, pre-finance, debts and liquidation must do everything possible to ensure that, even if there is no money in our coffers to pay civil servants' salaries, the soldiers must be paid on time. The last thing we want to hear or see is a soldier's hoof.

Notwithstanding all the efforts my government has been making – I have had to pay the soldiers from my personal national account abroad – some of the soldiers have been driven by blind ambition to want to shed our people's blood just because they want my throne. In this regard, I have no apology to make for arresting and eliminating the Wowo Trio for the mutiny 18 months ago and for engineering a wave of bombings. But for the vigilance of General Graffi Njanga and the rest of the army corps, this country would have been visited by untold human suffering.

A number of measures have had to be taken since I was sworn in for another term of office. They are intended to strengthen the hand of the president in his day-to-day dealings with members of the armed forces.

Being aware that tribalism is rife in my country, I decided to appoint heads of the different branches of our armed forces from different ethnic groups, especially from the main rival groups. The idea is that each one will spy on the other and report, out of jealousy, hate and spite, what the other is doing. In some cases, the key military staff I have appointed in the ministry of the armed forces are of junior rank as compared to their field commanders. This is very important because it will make for permanent bickering among them with the result that they will never come together in unity of purpose to stage a coup.

Also, as is done in every country in Africa, I appoint subservient officers in whom I have nothing but abiding trust to positions of influence in the armed forces. But then since in matters military trust is not enough, especially after soldiers discovered that the trigger can also be used to hoist themselves into the throne of president, I encourage senior officers to fight among themselves. This is done by promoting a junior officer to a higher rank above a deserving senior officer; assigning favourite officers to strategic duties, and encouraging them to spy on each other. It must be said that the policy has borne fruit and has also been responsible for my longevity in office.

Early this year, when I got word that General Mbin Shwiih was becoming very popular among his men, I appointed him as Mandzah's ambassador to far away Mbot. Once in a while I call him on the phone to tell him how much we miss him. It is important to make someone you know wants your place to feel that you respect him. I make him believe that he is the only senior military officer whom I trust and who has direct access to me. I must say Mbin Shwiih, being the exuberantly egoistic and power-hungry officer I know him to be, is greatly flattered.

There have been lots of speculation about my relationship with the air force, especially with Air Commodore Nahka. All I can say is that if I had had any quarrel with Nahka, I wouldn't have appointed him Air Commodore, and if he had anything against me, he wouldn't have accepted the national duty of bombing and strafing his own village following anti-government demonstrations and riots. I didn't ask him to decimate his people for nothing. Since he suffers from vaulting ambition, he has, by killing his own people, snuffed out his own dreams of ever using his ethnic group as a springboard to power.

In these times when rampant military takeovers are no longer very fashionable, and when reigning soldier-presidents are scheming to be civilian-presidents throughout Africa, most people have been speculating why my government has not yet been toppled when some have gone like houses built on sand. I must say if I am still in power and holding steady, it is not because enemies have not tried. There have been numerous unsuccessful attempts to oust me from power but each time I have outsmarted the enemies and eliminated them wholesale. I just have not been making too much noise about it as some of my colleagues have been doing.

Politicians

Politicians are well known for the effrontery with which they break promises. Unlike what some people may think, politicking is a profession. Thus, politicians, like other professionals, will go to any length to maintain themselves in power.

Everybody knows that politicians give the impression that their country comes first although their greatest consideration is their own survival as politicians. This is why they have to change positions on the same issue several times depending on the direction of the electoral wind.

When we achieved independence, I began an experiment with democracy and party politics that I thought would give every citizen a say in the way our country was being governed. Little did I know that I was giving politicians the ammunition with which to destroy the very ideals for which my party stood.

Bowing to popular pressure, I, with much regret, agreed that we should experiment rather with a single-party system to avoid the clans, the rift, and the dissensions that were undermining our development efforts. Politicians had become self-seeking, self-centred and power-drunk.

When parliamentary democracy gave way to our beloved single party which is an emanation of the public will, former politicians, nostalgic about the past and unhappy about their loss of power, began holding clandestine meetings to overthrow the popularly elected government over which I held sway. The party recommended that political parties be banned. I at first demurred but was forced through nationwide demonstrations and petitions to change my mind. I caved in to the will of the people. A good leader is one who knows how to do his people's will when it is convenient to him.

In defiance of our laws, former politicians have not ceased to embarrass government at will. Some of them have since fled abroad alleging that their lives are in danger. If their lives are indeed in danger, it is certainly not my government that threatened them but the people whom they have deceived for long. People have slowly come to realize that politicians keep on promising them goods they cannot deliver. When these politicians fall from power, the people want them to account for their misdeeds and misuse of power.

Our security services have been defending Mandzah and have not failed to identify those former politicians who have now elected to unduly criticize my government while offering nothing better but platitudes in return. My government has always been open to dialogue and has called for the full participation of every citizen in the political life of this nation. However, it is adamant that it will not yield to the blowing wind of senseless criticism, tirades and diatribe by self-styled politicians.

Because of the serious threat that politicians pose for the stability of my government and for the security of the state, we decided to reinforce the security of our country. Former politicians have been advised, in their own interest, to request security protection because of the incessant threats they face from the people. After banning the political parties, we realized that some former politicians were still very popular in their regions and even in the rest of the country because of the promises they had made to their constituencies: promises of jobs, scholarships, and development projects that they know they cannot fulfil.

I know a few former politicians who have bragged openly that I am not popular and that if there were a presidential election today, I would be defeated. I challenge any of them to obtain the 99.99% votes I have received in the past seven general elections. I even received 105 and 111.79% in two elections.

For over thirty years, my people have, on their own, every five years, entreated me to serve my country. Out of love for Mandzah, it is only normal that I should accept it, all the more as I am the only candidate they always propose. If I refuse, there will be no other popular leader.

The world knows the tremendous pressure to which I am subjected each time an election is around the corner. The whole country, through the different local and national party organs, massively starts demonstrating support for everything I have done. Then petitions follow: the armed forces, the ministries, ambassadors, students, farmers, trade unions, business people, in short, the entire country, sends delegations to beg me to stand as the only candidate that can unify the country, put the economy that I derailed back on the right track, and ensue sustainable development for our people. I usually have no choice but to bow to the people's wishes.

Until the security forces started rounding up some of the former politicians for their continued popularity, which is a violation of the age-old tradition that all popularity is vested in the president, I had had talks with a few of them and we agreed that they would keep a very low profile. But then a baboon's behind is always red. They persisted in maintaining their popularity and went to the extent of dropping hints that they were my friends and acting up as if they held the reins of power.

I do not know of any country in Africa in which popularity is not the exclusive preserve of the president. I, therefore, do not see why I should break with tradition.

The most noticeable former parliamentarian that was causing problems for my government is Aban Magaba whom we arrested when he was distributing money to some beggars along the Independence Avenue in his hometown of Ngomwumu. Our security people reported that Magaba had adopted the detestable habit of wearing flashy clothes, smoking a pipe, alighting from his splashy customized car in full view of everyone, and then summoning all the beggars to his car and distributing money to them. He was doing this purposely to maintain the aura of importance that he had when he was a member of the now defunct House of Representatives that I banned.

I was accused of arresting Magaba on trumped-up charges, but those who accuse me have not taken time to learn our traditional value systems and the laws that govern Mandzah's traditional way of life. It is not because we live in so-called modern times that we should abandon our traditions. Magaba's arrest and imprisonment will serve as a lesson to those like him who believe they can, in the name of modernity, flout our traditional laws.

Party militants

The survival of our political, and consequently our economic, social, and cultural institutions depends, to a large extent, on the effectiveness and efficiency of our party militants and the party machine. As guardians of the purity of our dogmas, it is they on whose frail shoulders rest the onerous task of indoctrinating our people, spying on them and, in the final analysis, ensuring the peace and stability of my government and the nation.

At the last party congress, the party was reorganized and party militants were given a very crucial role to play in reviving the dying embers of our nationalism, stoking the flame of our struggle for a just world order, and fanning the flame of hate and bitterness against our enemies.

As far as we are concerned, all citizens are party militants. They have always displayed their love for their country and for its president by organizing mammoth rallies throughout the length and breath of this nation to show to the world that they stand by me despite the hate campaign that has been launched from several quarters against me. But while acknowledging that all citizens are party militants, I must be candid and say we are not happy with the way some of the militants are behaving.

It is totally unacceptable to my government that while some militants show overt support for our institutions, they, at the same time, are showing covert support for our enemies both at home and abroad. Party militants cannot hope to walk with God and run with the devil.

We deplore the connivance of some of our militants with the forces of evil and destruction. How does one explain the fact that over the last few months alone the two military installations in our capital city have been bombed by unknown sources? We say because the party militants have not been vigilant enough. How come the minister of agriculture and food aid was ambushed, doused with petrol and set ablaze in broad daylight without any citizen coming forward as a witness to that dastardly act? We say because our party militants have been cowed by fear instead of being fortified by the spirit of patriotism.

All of us know that there is no disaffection with the policies that our party has adopted, and that the open, spontaneous and jubilant manifestation of loyalty that our people pledge to our national party and to me every year is living testimony of the esteem that we enjoy. It is in consideration of all these facts that the party and government decided to establish an effective espionage mechanism to ensure the surveillance of all party militants. Each militant was asked to be his brother's keeper.

Government Officials

One would have expected that since all senior government officials owe their station in life to me, they would give full backing to all government policies. But a few bad cocoyams are contaminating the rest. We know of government officials who are collaborating with our opponents by making available to them damaging government revelations that are used to drag the government's name in mud. Day in day out, confidential documents are leaked to the press and to our enemies. Some government officials grant interviews to the press under assumed names. Others give material and moral support to renegade politicians and plotters, and from within, many of them try, sometimes successfully, to sabotage the economy and government policies.

Early this year, at the height of the civil service strike, some top government functionaries were caught with inflammatory literature meant to stir our people's emotions and to cause panic and instability. Luckily for the government, the dreaming schemers were arrested before their so-called manifesto was circulated. They will pay a heavy price for betraying their country.

Last month, there was grumbling within the civil service union that employment conditions are shoddy; that salaries are not paid on time and that, in view of galloping inflation, salaries should match those in the private sector.

My government said at the time that it will not yield to any pressure group. Civil servants, more than any other group in this country, should know the harrowing conditions under which we are working, and thus not make demands that they know government cannot meet. They are in charge of the day-to-day operation of government and should be defending government policy instead of championing the cause of the nitwit opportunistic politicians.

Maybe most people do no fully grasp the extent to which our economy has been suffering. I wish to mention some of the major economic, cultural and social projects that have had to be scrapped for the time being because we have had to pare down the budget:

1. Renovation of my mother's country home in Alabukut.
2. Purchase of another presidential aircraft to add to the 2 other presidential crafts. It is no secret that the 2 aircrafts have become too small for my family and the security people that accompany me. Consequently, my son is using them to fly his mother on weekend shopping sprees in Tubab. Since the 4 helicopters are still in running order, we have not deemed it necessary to purchase new ones. However, the landing strip on top of the People's House needs reconditioning. A president needs to be able to fly out at a moment's notice if he is being chased out in a national emergency.
3. Reduction of the amounts transferred abroad to our personal national bank account. I know that this decision will be most unpopular because, if anything, it is during times of severe economic hardships that we should be transferring money abroad to save for the rainy day. But the government has no choice, and I hope my people will understand our predicament. I wish to assure them that as soon as the new budget is passed, and as soon as we receive the development assistance funds we requested from donors, we shall immediately replenish my foreign bank accounts. Everyone knows that there is no money in the country because

depositors no longer have confidence in our banking system and are sending their money abroad.

4. Curtailment of official visits abroad. I have decided that because of the beleaguered state of the economy, I shall drastically reduce the number of visits planned for this year. Instead of attending all the noisy regional meetings, I shall visit as many Tubab countries as possible. We need to keep our Tubab backers fully informed of all the underdevelopment projects we are undertaking with their money. We also need to pander to the international press and explain that underdevelopment aid money is used for the purpose for which it was intended. We use money from our normal budget to enhance massive corruption and influence peddling. Also, we need more sophisticated arms to keep our armed forces trigger-happy and our enemies at bay. There are many things developing countries need. For example, we need a massive dose of food aid to douse the political flames ignited by the furor of the restive farmers in Tubab, and we have to allay the fears of the world about the secret executions project we implemented last year. We do not want to give room to Tubab public opinion to boot those officials who are backing us out of office. Tubab elections are not far away. Already, Charlie Quoiquoi of the Romance Republic, recently visited Romance-speaking Africa's bloodthirsty dictators to collect blood money from them for his election campaign in exchange for promises to maintain the dictators in power.

5. While the armed forces will receive the pay increase they requested and all the weapons and ammunition we promised them, we shall postpone the renovation work on the armed forces' central cemetery. We do not anticipate any mutiny or war this year nor do we intend to fake another military coup soon. Most of the politicians and armed forces personnel whom we would normally accuse have only been recently released form maximum-security prison following the fake coup three yeas ago.

6. We have suspended the decision to substantially increase the number of ministries. We think that 50 ministries as we have them now is more than adequate to implement our self-

reliant, self-sustaining underdevelopment policy. However, in order to ensure accountability and a narrowing down of regional disparities, we have decided to increase the number of political divisions and divisional officers from five to fifteen, and to give each divisional officer ministerial rank.

7. I have, with immediate effect, instructed the managing directors of the Mengyen Oil Corporation, the Metah Timber Corporation, the Menjah Realty Corporation, the Oga and Oga Food Distributors Ltd., the Mebah Electronics Company, the Mambei Meat and Fish Suppliers, the Widekumat Brothers Transport Company, the Allied Industries Ltd., the Ngumba Hotels and Resort Corporation and the National Mining Development Company to deposit my own share of this year's profits into government coffers. The other members of my family have also decided to surrender the profits from their worldwide investments to the national treasury as their own way of bailing the country out of the economic recession.

8. We are pleading with the party and all the traditional chiefs to accept the postponement of the celebration of my father's death anniversary until the economy has bounced back to life. All monies so far collected will be deposited into my personal national account and all gifts sold. The nation will be informed in due course of the new date for the ceremony so that new contributions and gifts can be made.

9. Work on the building of the independence monument featuring my bust has been called to a temporary halt. With our economy under siege, I think we can postpone exposing my bust.

10. All subsidies paid by government to our farmers are hereby suspended until the budgetary situation improves. In taking this measure, we have already taken necessary precautions to ensure that there will continue to be a bumper supply of food aid.

It was our hope that these comprehensive solutions to the agonizing and staggering problems that face us will result in easing the problems and making available boundless opportunities for development.

Traditional Rulers

I have always maintained that our traditions are sacred, and that we should try to blend the past with the present, the modern with the traditional.

The foundation on which our society is sitting is cast in the concrete of our traditional values. Our traditional rulers ought therefore to be the cultural ambassadors of our society. Unfortunately, partly out of greed and partly out of lust for power, they have become more westernized than any of us.

I have no regrets that I banned the House of Chiefs because, instead of using it as a forum to discuss how to cooperate with government, our traditional rulers used it as a springboard to rise to power and to challenge everything we were doing. In my inaugural address to the chiefs when I took over the mantle of leadership of our people, I assured them that I would work closely with them to improve the lot of our rural citizens who constitute the bulk of the population. They pledged their support and loyalty to me.

Barely four years after that solemn promise, our traditional rulers started refusing to implement government policy and became increasingly interested in politics. They no longer collected taxes as vigorously as they did before and even encouraged law-abiding citizens to disobey government orders. Attempts to bring them to reason failed.

It wasn't long before the die was cast. The House of Chiefs petitioned the government to reduce taxes in certain cases and to waive them altogether for certain classes of citizens. I responded that the House should mind its own business and leave national issues to the national government. Chiefs were only to be responsible for their villages. In a fit of aggravating exasperation, the House voted to take government to court for not recognizing its right to represent the people.

My immediate reaction was to ban it. I did not believe at the time, nor do I now, that the courts have anything to do with purely political issues. After all, I am the one who appoints judges.

Since the banning of the House of Chiefs, chiefs have been conspiring to thwart our development efforts. For example, I used to visit His Highness Chief Lekumbeng regularly for consultations because he is known throughout the country as the foremost traditional doctor. Even white people flock to him to seek counseling to solve their matrimonial and other problems.

In some cases, jilted white men go to him to win back their wives who ran away with their black cook or driver. In other cases, the white men go to him to cook medicine so that they can remain indefinitely in Mandzah and not return to their country in Tubab to be subjected to the rigours of harsh winters, competition for jobs, and a generally more difficult life.

When I last visited Chief Lekumbeng, I decided there and then to ban the House of Chiefs. Unbeknownst to me prior to my visits to him, while Chief Lekumbeng made me believe that he served exclusively as my private witch doctor, he at the same time was the witch doctor of one of my country's deadliest enemies, Mr. Dongfawo, who was the centrifugal opposition force against me. Although Lekumbeng denied ever revealing to my political nemeses what we discussed in private, or the fact that I used to visit him to obtain medicine to neutralize my political enemies in order to remain in power for as long as I wanted, I started to have misgivings about Lekumbeng and to distrust native doctors generally.

I was comforted in my distrust when I saw the same walking stick and cap that Lekumbeng had tailor-made for my protection with Dr. Kwacha Mimbo, minister of contracts in the MIP's shadow cabinet.

As I look back on those events now, I begin to understand why my opponents forestalled every trap I set for them and every move I made. Attempts on my part to implicate members of the MIP in all the treasonable crimes being committed against my government usually took a very long time to succeed.

After giving serious consideration to the unpatriotic acts of the traditional rulers, and after discussing the matter with some party militants, I decided that if I did not put a leash on the traditional rulers, they might not know the metes and bounds of their mandate.

I do not know how some warped minds have successfully peddled information round the world that I ordered the arrest and execution of some chiefs. I have no knowledge that any chief was executed on my orders. My government has been cooperating fully with the chiefs in maintaining peace and order and in identifying development projects.

Recently, I invited all the paramount chiefs to the People's House and we spoke freely, openly and frankly about our common problems. As part of my commitment to a policy of unstrained dialogue with all segments of our society, the chiefs and I discussed a number of priority activities that should be undertaken immediately throughout the country.

1. Beefing up security in the village because the roaming band of discontented and disenchanted politicians sowing wild political oats poses a severe threat to the lives of our rural people.
2. Purchasing a car for each chief who co-operates fully with us. This issue of motorable roads was raised, but at the time, it was the government's view that first things should be tackled first. The cars were to be purchased and, as funds became available, the roads would be repaired. Our view then, as it is now, is that in times of economic crisis, we must get our priorities right.
3. In order to ease the tremendous burden of farming activities on our farmers, we decided to give our farmers a three-year's respite. The co-operatives were advised in their own interest not to buy any produce for the next three years, and the security of our borders strengthened to prevent any cross-border trade. Given the stockpile of locally produced food in warehouses throughout the country, and given the over-abundance of imported foods on our markets, there is really no need for our farmers to take their farm work too seriously.
4. We reject outright the suggestion that markets and farm-to-market roads be built on the premise that if our Five-Year Plan is going to be well implemented, there will be no need for markets or for these roads as there will be nothing to market in the rural areas.

Students

Students in Mandzah are a privileged bunch. My government recognizes that the future of our country lies in the hands of our youth. For this reason, we have gone out of our way, especially in these times of national crisis, to ensure a good educational foundation for our children who are tomorrow's Mandzahs.

While recognizing the pre-eminent place of our youth in our struggle for development, we should not get carried away by the ranting of a few students who have turned going to school a profession.

We have witnessed over the years a growing restlessness among our students since we allowed students to engage in politics on school campuses. In our attempt to give a voice to our students and thus prepare them for the political chores of tomorrow, we painstakingly, and at great cost, set up a party school for young party cadres.

We are happy that the party school has lived up to expectations. Each year the school receives thousands and thousands of applications from parents who identify with our ideals and want their children to be indoctrinated. The indoctrination classes we organize have been so successful that during my last cabinet reshuffle, I appointed Nyam Ngup as the minister of special duties. Part of his assignment is to ensure that our young party cadre receive the best indoctrination possible. Mr. Nyam Ngup is himself an alumnus of the school and is very familiar with its methods.

While we are doing our best to provide the best form of leadership for our country, some individuals from the university who think they are more intelligent than we are have been bent on causing tremendous havoc to our youth. Instead of taking their lessons seriously, students would flock out of class, assemble on the steps of the minister of education. Illiteracy and re-education's office and taunt and insult him. I would like to take this opportunity to thank the minister for his patience and forbearance. If this had happened in another African country, all the students would have been eliminated. We eliminated just a few.

We in Mandzah fervently believe in giving people a second chance. We have thus tried to negotiate with our students, but they have construed our love for dialogue as a sign of weakness. The students have been complaining that the quality of their food is poor; that they must all be on scholarship; that they must all pass at the end of the school year, and that I must fire my minister of education, illiteracy and re-education. These are, of course, indirect attacks on my person.

The international press has recently, as is its wont, been up in arms against our people as it usually does when it listens to one-sided arguments. Thank God our local press is mature enough and refused to comment on stories it can neither confirm nor deny.

We are proud of our free press record. All we ask of our press is that it publish the truth based on our pronouncements and on the briefings by the ministry of information, disinformation, propaganda and censorship. Recently, when the students went on strike to protest because of the poor quality of their food, the minister of education, illiteracy and re-education set up a committee to probe into the affair. The committee, the Nyamangoro Committee, so named after its venerable chairman, the former chief cook and butler in the Grass Fields Intercontinental Hotel, Gwi Nyamangoro, made a number of recommendations.

The committee found out that the contractor supplying the food was the minister himself, and recommended that I sack him. I am still studying the report and will tell the nation what measures will be taken to right the situation.

I do not believe a committee has the right to dictate to me whom to appoint or fire because that will be a dangerous precedent. I would be opening the floodgate of retribution and lighting the fire that will destroy our political vegetation as we know it.

Throughout this episode, I realized that some of my people have not yet woken up to the sacrificial services that some of us are rendering our country. The accused minister of education, illiteracy and re-education, Mr. Ngwa Soya, is an illiterate that has been performing his duties with selfless devotion to duty. Ngwa Soya has been with me since colonial times and has borne with me the brunt of the insults that our thankless job has brought us. I do not think it is fair for any group of individuals to ask me to fire him just because of a few missing bags of ice, cartons of sardines and tomatoes.

I wish to be quite clear because students have adopted the habit of always asking for the head of a minister they don't like, especially when they feel like abandoning classes to roam about the streets in the name of a demonstration. I sincerely don't know what they are demonstrating except their immaturity and greed.

First, as an equal opportunity President, I cannot fire any of the key illiterate members of my government. Let that be heard far and wide. Ngwa Soya has proven to be one of the most successful ministers in my cabinet. He is one of those who read the manuscript of this historical book and made wonderful suggestions for its improvement. Of course, I refused to entertain the suggestions. I know of hundreds of so-called intellectuals in or country that have absolutely nothing to show for their great learning.

Second, I am the President of this Republic and I, and I alone can decide when and how I want to eliminate my ministers. In this I don't need anybody's assistance.

Third, we do not want to create the situation where any aggrieved group can give itself the liberty of petitioning to me for every problem that needs to be solved.

Furthermore, Ngwa Soya has been accused of being tribalistic. As far as I know, most of the university lecturers are from his ethnic region, but this is precisely because if he chose people from some and not all the ethnic groups, people would accuse him of tribalism. As we strive to build one nation indivisible, we should avoid those actions that will divide our people.

Let me now discuss a few problems that have plagued our educational system.

Rumours have been spread by our enemies worldwide that, in quelling the student demonstration that took place four months ago, my soldiers shot indiscriminately at poor defenseless students. I say that is hogwash. The press, which claims to be so knowledgeable about everything, should have done its homework. In the first place, it was a battle between two opposing forces. The students were armed to the teeth with slogans, petitions and fiery speeches while my soldiers only had armoured cars, tanks, guns, truncheons, tear gas and long drawn out penises to defend themselves against the blighted fury of the massive student crowd.

Also, our soldiers are well trained and were very discriminating. They did not, as has been alleged, shoot indiscriminately at students. They shot the students they had targeted. There is therefore no truth to the statement that stray bullets hit some students and bystanders. Our soldiers are excellent marksmen although General Bandeh Tandeh tried unsuccessfully to assassinate me last year. He was executed for being a sloppy marksman.

It is also a blatant and outright lie that there was a massacre of student protesters. It always bids my imagination how, even though we banned the foreign press from covering the demonstration, it could stoop so low as to disseminate information about something it does not know, especially without first checking with us.

To set the record straight, let the world know that there was never a massacre of students in my country. We did not fight against Hitler's tyranny to institute that kind of a regime in this country. I expect the press, given the educational role it plays in society, to be better informed and careful in its choice of words and presentation of facts.

Political opponents

Politics is one profession in which the mediocre excel. One only has to look round the world to see that politics is the triumph of money over ideas. I know of no statesman that has not been vilified even when he gave of himself selflessly to the cause of his people. And because politics is a fertile field in which bread and butter issues are grown, anyone believes that he can be a political farmer.

I have cultivated politics from childhood, and I know the various types of soils in which a political seed sown today will bloom into a thriving political plant tomorrow.

There have been several disgruntled elements in Mandzah since I started reigning as President. I have already discussed some of them here and there and would not like to give them more importance than they truly deserve. My government believes in constructive criticism and not in diabolical and malicious slander intended to thwart our inexorable march toward development.

We have extended a hand of friendship to our enemies who are residing abroad, far from the realities at home, and invited them to return and join us in building a prosperous nation. While some of them have returned and apologized to the people for insulting them, others have continued to shell out a steady stream of destabilizing criticism against us. In some cases, the ringleaders have not been to this country in over twenty years although they claim to know what is happening in our country on a day-to-day basis.

I am aware that some of my ministers and other officials of government are in the habit of disclosing confidential information and government secrets to these ideological orphans. I am also aware that these so-called revolutionaries, who claim to love this country more than we do, and who believe they have all the answers to our problems, are nothing but glorified opportunists. Some of them are students who went abroad on government scholarship and instead of studying, fell into the warm lap of Tubab women. When we withdrew their scholarships, they joined the opposition and instead of telling the world the truth, they say we withdrew the scholarships because they were our political enemies. And they get a sympathetic hearing from some misguided Tubab quarters. Others are former government officials fleeing from justice at home.

We do not doubt the sincerity of some of the self-styled revolutionaries. Their faith in this country is total and their criticisms genuine. In fact, I read all their tracts, and listen to their criticisms. Some of them, however, join the opposition because they want jobs back home. We know them. We have discovered that whenever a young Mandzah national abroad wants a plum job back home, he immediately joins the opposition so we can notice him. When we finally entice him with a job and he returns home, he then shuts up.

I know of no Mandzah so-called revolutionary who has, in keeping with the dictates of revolutionary command, refused a plum job we offered him. And because all of them are looking homewards for a good position in government, they keep on betraying each other to us. I have several files with letters we have been receiving from some of the most vociferous revolutionaries apologizing to us that they were misled by so and so and asking for our forgiveness. They usually end the letter by asking us if they can return home to help us build the country. What they really mean is that they are tired of living abroad and doing menial jobs to survive, and that they now want to return home to build their bank accounts.

All this goes to show that we are not in the least scared of the dismembered opposition that thrives abroad on hearsay. We have absorbed most of them in our government and given them the opportunity to implement the fertile ideas they claimed to have when they were abroad.

We are not aware that any of them has put forward any bright idea to extricate us from the economic morass that is paralyzing Mandzah or from the political ferment that we are witnessing. All of them are fighting to survive, and that is what is wrong with Africa. No so-called Mandzah revolutionary is prepared to die for a cause, not even for his or her own cause.

I do not need to refer the reader to the number of fire-breathing revolutionaries that were given militant support by some Tubab countries to fight against their motherland. They crisscrossed continents preaching hate, revolution, and war, but when it came down to the nitty gritty, they, all to a man, after suffering indignity of the average Tubab's scorn, and lack of popularity at home, returned to accept positions in the very government they spent their lives criticizing. When they are given key positions, they acquiesce and perpetrate, with a vengeance, the same policies they had been criticizing from abroad. I say I have nothing but irreverent disrespect and contempt for all African so-called revolutionaries hanging out in the cold in Tubab.

13

Indoctrination

Immediately our enemies, or as they are called in the language of politics, revolutionaries, return home after spending years in the cold abroad, they are interviewed by a panel made up of a judge, a member of the armed forces, an official of the national security, a university professor, and officials of the party. They are grilled on their past activities, and supporters at home. This interview is akin to an entrance examination because it determines the class into which they will be put in the party school.

If the self-styled revolutionary is well versed in revolutionary rote thinking and knows all the common revolutionary expressions and slogans, he is admitted in class 1 and so on. In other words, the more sophisticated the revolutionary, the longer it will take him to graduate because it will take longer to brainwash him. There are 20 classes in the school and promotion to a new class is on the basis of performance. Most revolutionaries repeat some classes and thus take more than the normal 20 years to graduate. On the other hand, some of the very dull ones who probably joined the opposition simply to cover up their academic weaknesses, are immediately put in higher classes to graduate faster. It is easier to transform these dull ones into intelligent citizens than it is to transform the intelligent revolutionaries.

The syllabus of the party school is well designed to take into account not only the various schools of philosophical, political and economic thought, but also the changing realities of Mandzah. The core courses are civics, my political thoughts, civics, my political thoughts, civics, my political thoughts, and finally, civics and my political thoughts. The optional courses, which all students must take, are indoctrination, civics, and my political thoughts. Classes begin from 7:00 a.m. to 6 p.m. from Monday to Sunday.

At the end of their program, successful graduates are awarded plum jobs in government or in the private sector. My current minister of investigations and cover up, Rev. Chakara Bambe, graduated summa cum laude from the school in a record 18 years instead of the normal 20. Prior to attending the party school, he had obtained a degree in theology from the well-known Mission University of Promiseland, and joined the defunct Mandzah Revolutionary command (MAREC) in Tubab and became its president.

As minister of investigations and cover up, Rev. Bambe's training in both theology and indoctrination come in handy. He chairs the National Security Committee that recruits candidates into the party school, and since he, more than any one else, knows how the school functions, he chooses the right calibre of students for the school.

Mr. Nguket Yawe, managing director of the Mandzah Marketing Board, was also a graduate of the party school. He spent only 5 years there because he was admitted into class 15. He, like Bambe, had been a member of MAREC, but unlike Bambe, he had quit university in first year to drive taxis. Today he is responsible for monitoring the performance of the various marketing boards.

There are many other members of my government that were visceral opponents of our policies. In the name of national unity and reconciliation, we welcomed all of them wholeheartedly into our fold after their graduation from the party school.

14

Disinformation

We define disinformation as publishing or broadcasting false information to counter false information. There is no reason why we should cross our arms and not react when our enemies, be they individuals, groups, or countries, publish or broadcast false information with the avowed aim of tarnishing our good name. I do not see why the Tubabs should be allowed to have a controlling interest in the disinformation industry when we have all the resources that can give us an edge in this sector.

Disinformation is a staple food on the tables of all governments, irrespective of political stripe. We therefore do not claim any originality for the disinformation ideas that we have adopted.

In fact, disinformation comes in many forms, some of which are so obvious that nobody pays attention to them. For example, state-owned newspapers, and even some private ones, are fronts for political parties; so too are trade unions, business tycoons, governments, radio and television, etc. Even researchers and scientists sometimes engage in a little disinformation. At any rate, disinformation is not the exclusive preserve of any particular country.

My government has used and will continue to use various media to thwart those who are bent on sowing the seed of confusion among our people. I shall give a few examples to show how our enemies have been waging a relentless disinformation war of attrition against us.

Last year when there was a riot in the People's Stadium during a football match between the Nap football team that we had invited to take part in our Independence Day celebrations and our national team, the Vultures, there was a media ballyhoo all over the world. The international press announced that 11 people had died. No one had bothered to check with us to ascertain the right number of victims. Nor had any journalist taken the time to go to the People's Hospital to find out from the emergency department.

For the record, there were about 76 dead and 187 missing. We do not have an accurate record of the number of spectators that were crammed in the stadium that day, but our sports officials estimate that there must have been about 80,000 spectators in the 30,000 capacity stadium. An investigation is underway and the press will be thoroughly briefed in due course.

A few months ago a Tubab journalist who had come to our country masquerading as a tourist reported that my darling wife had moved out of the presidential mansion (the People's House), and gone back to her family because I was frolicking with a female member of my cabinet. I say the press should be responsible and publish only facts. If it wishes to publish rumours, it should consult with me.

The truth is that Dzo and I fought. I hurt my knuckles and she broke her jaw. But she did not go back to her family. She moved into the guest presidential villa behind the People's House and the female cabinet minister moved into her room.

Last month the Tubab security people, in their usual bid to discredit my government, accused my minister of social welfare, Mrs. Wayo Moyo, of being a drug dealer. We know that Mrs. Moyo and her husband, Cain, like some officials of my government, smoke grass from time to time. These things happen everyday all over the world. But smoking a few herbs and trafficking in drugs are two different activities.

Worse, a decent woman like Mrs. Moyo was said to have hidden the grass in her private parts and bandaged it to make it appear that she was seeing her period.

Given the serious charges against Mrs. Moyo, I sent one of my sons, Adzinep Wan Nei, my special adviser on national and state matters, to go and meet with both the Tubab security people and Mrs. Moyo herself. It turned out that the Tubab security officials had once again exaggerated.

It is true that Mrs. Moyo had wrapped the stuff around her waist. Certainly, there is an anatomical and functional difference between one's waist and one's private parts. But what right did the Tubab security people have to be prying into a woman's private parts? We say civilized society must live by the norms of civilized society.

My special adviser also confirmed that Mrs. Moyo admitted to carrying 3 kilograms of the stuff, but contrary to the disinformation of the Tubab security people, she said she was carrying it for her own use and not for sale.

She is also reported to have willingly opened her thighs to show the customs people that she had nothing to hide. From what I know of her, she has never hidden her private parts from anybody who wanted to see them. Yet the Western press published banner headlines about a Mandzah minister who had hidden drugs in her private parts.

The most disingenuous disinformation campaign ever launched against our people came from neighbouring Nap, a barren country with a president just as barren and bereft of fertile ideas. We have opened our doors wide to Napians to come and eke an existence in our country. We have, at great cost to our people, agreed to sell food to them at much reduced prices. Yet we are the butt of their insults, political intrigues and machinations.

The Nap national radio, the Voice of Nap, is its master's voice. All its broadcasts are gratuitous attacks against us for no reason. When something happens in Mandzah, they claim to know it all and announce lies and fabricated stories to the world about what, in their villainous scheme, actually took place. And the Western press, ever so gullible, ever so sensational, picks up the half-baked can of lies and feeds it to its people who do not know any better. Then their politicians, who are always looking elsewhere but home for a straw to hang onto, clutch to the drivel and turn it into political electoral phrases.

What happened two years ago is something that we in this country will never forget. I had never before, in my entire political career, crossed the ecstatic frontier of hate. With the surrogate Butibun of Nap, I confess that I crossed that frontier.

Butibun had amassed troops along our common border in the hope of striking at the heart of our farming regions and destroying our enterprising agricultural sector. As cowards usually do, he decided to announce to the world that the invasion was going to be launched by my opponents. He accused me of supporting the rebel Nap Democratic Front that was contesting his right to govern.

Everyone knows that the tongue of a liar is always sweet. The international media allowed itself to be cajoled into believing the story and defended Butibun's right to attack us without probing. The African Solidarity Union said it would sit on the fence to see which side it would support after we had destroyed each other. But for my calmness and maturity, I would have led my people into a deadly and costly war that would have brought us nothing.

We have no ambition for territorial aggrandizement, and even if we wanted more territory, it would not be barren Nap. When the history books are written, historians will look back to that year as the year in which maturity triumphed over blind and selfish ambition. Needless to say arms dealers from all over the world were disappointed that I had refused to call Butibun's bluff.

They sent out untrue news about my cowardice and how we would have been wiped out in one single attack. I accept that form of humiliation if it means saving my country and people from waging a fratricidal war against my neighbours just because of the miscalculations of their deranged leader.

The ignominious tyranny of war is worse than any other form of tyranny. We want Butibun and others like him who are looking for foreign adventures abroad to kindle their people's spirit of nationalism, to know that we shall not back down in the future if they mass troops again at our borders.

As I blame Butibun, I must also caution his backers, those not so invisible hands that are cheering and egging him to attack my country and its people. Butibun has not yet understood that if I raze his villages and towns to the ground and drive him underground, the same people backing him now will be the same ones that will forfeit his country's meagre resources.

15

Favouritism and Nepotism

I do not need to define what favouritism and nepotism mean because everyone readily recognizes them. My country has come perilously close to disaster because my ministers and all those in important positions allowed these isms to fester and stand in the way of our development process. We have therefore put our hunting dog on the trail of those officials of my government who believe they can maintain themselves in their positions through favouritism and nepotism. I shall deal with tribalism in a separate chapter because it is slowly eating away our national fabric.

I am not aware of any government that countenances favouritism and nepotism. Yet, whenever those whose avowed aim is to vilify us take to the streets in the quest for publicity, they tax us with maintaining and fostering favouritism, nepotism and tribalism.

My government's efforts to rid Mandzah of these damaging scourges are well known. Our record is impeccable and any serious-minded person will see that although abolishing favouritism and nepotism is not an easy undertaking, we in Mandzah have successfully reined in the problem.

I wish to address myself to specific instances in which we have been falsely accused by the local and international media, including our detractors, of encouraging rampant corruption, favouritism and nepotism.

My family

I do not recall when, in blessed memory, any day has passed without someone somewhere casting aspersions on the good name of my family. People are behaving childishly as if I should not have had a family in the first place. Not only have I sired children throughout the length and breadth of this country, I have done so with women from all our tribes, and even with women in foreign countries that I visit. Our colleagues, in keeping with the elementary principle of hospitality, know that one's guests must be made to feel at home. I don't know if anyone in this country will ever match or break my record.

I believe I have not hidden it from the world that I have five wives: one is official and the others are something else. I have never made any bones about the fact that, like most Africans, I have a number of official children and a host of unofficial ones strewn all over the country. My life is an open book, and everyone knows what I am doing.

All our people know that because I am the President, every woman wants to claim ownership of my sentiments. Who isn't aware, for example, that every time a child is born somewhere, including the remotest parts of our country that I have never visited, news goes round that it is my child and the parents give them my name.

I am really astonished that whenever two or more people are gathered together, my family is the subject of discussions and speculation. I wish to clear the air once and for all.

Among my 23 official children (19 boys and 4 girls), the most well known is Genesis who was appointed minister of state in the Presidency immediately after he returned home from Tubab after dropping out of school.

Before I say anything about Genesis, let me make it clear that when he was in Tuba, he had the best facilities to study but he refused to go to school. He was on full scholarship like the children of my ministers and party luminaries. In addition, he had a very handsome allowance to enable him live in a penthouse and buy the sports cars he loved. Unlike what most parents think, his mother and I decided that it was good for him to start learning about life early.

We also encouraged Genesis to go out with girls of all nationalities, especially white girls who were fascinated by his being the son of an African president. Genesis organized regular parties in his penthouse to which he invited buddies with whom he hung out every night in the various chic nightclubs. We believed at the time and still do that children must be allowed to grow up on their own.

When Genesis was deported for involvement in drug dealing and stealing credit cards, our national party appointed him its deputy chairman against my own protests. I wanted him to be an independent businessman and consultant because it is a very lucrative field, especially if one is lucky to land a juicy contract. However, I was later on forced to appoint him as minister of state in the Presidency because our party kingpins said I needed to groom my successor.

As a minister of state, Genesis coordinated the activities of all the other ministries and also went on errands for his country. He was usually sent on missions to attend royal weddings and death ceremonies throughout the world. Since there is always some death ceremony somewhere in the world, Genesis was perpetually busy.

There is also Isaiah who recently accepted to serve his country in the most strategic position. After serving for several years as chairman of our National Utilities Corporation (NUC), Isaiah was appointed Army Chief of Staff. Prior to being the chairman of NUC, Isaiah had successfully graduated from the 6-month national military training program where he trained as a General.

As the patriot that he was, Isaiah accepted to continue holding on to his other assignments although he was overwhelmed with his duties as Commanding General. He is concurrently chairman of the Board of Mandzah National Railways Corporation, president of the Chamber of Commerce, Industry and Agriculture, chief patron of the Mandzah Association of the Handicapped, chairman of the Sports Council and secretary of the African Ministerial Committee on Debts and Loans. Our country was recently honoured when Isaiah was appointed the first chairman of the International Federation for the Promotion of Alcohol and Tobacco. He recently attended the inaugural meeting of the newly formed Committee of Western Countries to support African Dictators.

I believe a president and his family must be imbued with a high sense of patriotism, and be seen as giving of themselves selflessly to the cause of their country. I therefore believe it is only fair and normal that my immediate family should be serving the country the way it is doing in various positions so that our people will wake up to the essence of the work ethic that I have tried to inculcate in them over the years.

My family is proud of the services it is rendering Mandzah, and expects the rest of the population to do likewise. A few years ago, I appointed my youngest son, Proverbs, as the ambassador to Criton, much against his will. Proverbs had turned down several job offers on the pretext that he was too young. Of course, Proverbs wasn't that young as he claimed. He was 22 and simply wanted to be flying the presidential jet all over the world. But even if he was young, it is well known that, in royal families, minors can be kings or queens.

When my family met to discuss what to do with Proverbs, it was decided that if Proverbs couldn't, at 22, understand the noble mission that destiny and the nation had assigned to my family, we would have to teach him by force. And that's exactly what we did. The government decided that an ambassadorial post would prepare him well for that of foreign minister.

Like every family, my family also has its black sheep. I would have liked to gloss over this subject but it will be out of character. While asserting that my family must be in the vanguard championing the cause of our beloved country, I must say that I am disappointed in my other official children, including the four girls.

Let me talk about the girls first since nothing good, it seems, will ever come out of them. My daughters have not been taking their studies seriously, and despite all my efforts, they have refused to accept important positions in government under the pretext that they are not qualified. I have asked them to look at their brothers, my ministers and many of my appointees to see the tremendous work they are doing for their country, but they will not listen. They claim that all these people are doing a disservice to Mandzah because nothing good seems to come out of them.

Needless to say, I am disappointed in my girls just as I know the nation too is. I am particularly distraught because of Ruth who is loved by everyone. We all thought she would like to be the secretary-general of the women's wing of our national party since her mother is the president, but she turned it down. As if their disloyalty to the country was not enough, all my girls refused to get married to the men recommended by the family. Their argument is that they are big enough to do what they please and to marry whoever they wish.

My consolation, and I guess it should also be the nation's, is that my daughters are still young and probably do not know what they are doing. But the problem is that, by the time they reach 30, they may be too old to occupy any important positions in my government since I might not be around given the violent winds of change that are blowing across Africa.

With regard to the other official boys, they have decided that since they are not doing well at school, business is their calling. It seems to be the case that not doing well at school is an affliction of the children of the rich and famous.

Job and Jeremiah have been given a $10 million loan by our Central Bank to start their own business. From the look of things, the business is already booming. They have bought up choice land and property in the posh government residential area where they hope to break down all the houses to build their office complex. In the mean time, they have already purchased everything they need from office furnishings to the latest communications gear. I am excited to see my children setting out on their own without any backing from me or anybody.

As for Akere and Goliath who are still tied at home with their mother, they have decided to eat, drink and be merry. I do not think I will allow them stay at home for too long. Luckily for them, the minister of transport offered Akere the position of chief pilot with the Mandzah National Airways but he turned it down because he gets to see the same places free of charge with his mother. Goliath is negotiating with a Tubab Five company to sell military hardware. It appears that the minister of defense has already assured him that he will be awarded all government contracts to purchase arms and ammunition for our armed forces. Apparently trade in arms is a very lucrative business although I fear for his business because one has the eerie feeling that people are sick and tired of war. If the need arises, I am sure we can always obtain the backing of the Western world to start some war somewhere. Alternatively, the Western world may encourage us to fight among ourselves to sell their arms.

I do not wish to give people the mistaken impression that this is all of my family. Of course, this can't be all of it. One of the most distinguishing cultural features between Tubabs and us is our extended family system. In addition to my official children, there are the unofficial ones as well as cousins, nephews and nieces who are known throughout the country because of the key positions they occupy in government and in the private sector. They need no introduction.

With regard to my other official wife, Shilambe (High Life) Shiri, the low profile she has been keeping has sparked lots of unfounded rumours about the stability of our marriage. The world and the press in particular should be informed that we have been happily married for over 40 years and are a happy family. We are neither members of a constitutional monarchy nor members of the jet-set society to be swapping wives or changing partners everyday.

My state wife, the Mother of the Nation, decided alone, after I forced her, that since her position as president of the woman's wing of our great national party is too demanding of her time, she will spend what little time she has left to helping our business people compete with the foreigners who control our economy. It is a sad reflection on our country that even though I do not interfere in what my appointees do with the money they embezzle, foreigners continue to dominate every sector of our business and commercial life.

When I told my ministers several years ago that my government encourages foreign investments, they thought that by foreign investment I was encouraging them to transfer all their wealth abroad. The International Loan Shark Fund gave us a loan to invite a well-known international Tubab investment firm, Gerald, George and Grit (The Three Gees), to visit our country and explain what we meant to our people.

The representatives of Gerald, George and Grit made it quite clear that since our country was broke (although our nationals have stashed away lots of money in vaults abroad), they would provide all the experts they felt we needed as long as we allowed them to repatriate all the money paid them by the International Loan Shark Fund. Our government officials were so happy that they sent delegations to congratulate The Three Gees for their assistance in under developing our country.

My state wife, for her part, embarked on a number of business deals that should, in the very near future, give business and economic power to our people. At the moment, she has established a private corporation (with some Tubab businessmen) to control the import and export of key products. She hopes to serve as an intermediary between all local and foreign business people operating in this country. The idea is that no one should be able to import or export anything without going through her and paying the mandatory commissions.

She has also become involved in the key agricultural sector. We will soon ban the marketing board so that she can have the monopoly of marketing all our produce. We feel constrained to take this measure because of the failure of the marketing board to pay our farmers on time and to obtain favourable world prices for their produce.

Finally, a few months ago, she came up with another brilliant business idea. She said she would be contacting all ministers, directors, heads of state-owed enterprises, and so on, to contribute money towards the establishment of a Mandzah Business Promotion Foundation. She has already been very instrumental in establishing many foundations in our country. The most well known are the Gold and Diamonds Recovery Foundation, the Breadbasket Foundation to sell food aid, the Privatization Foundation to collect the commissions being paid by foreign companies which want to buy up our thriving industries, the Women's Advisory Foundation to organize political support for the government and to recommend which deserving men should be appointed to senior positions, and the Welcome Foundation to manage the budget allocated to the entertainment of visiting delegations.

My wife does not want Mandzah to lag behind other countries in any sector because, throughout the world, every president's wife is championing some cause.

My Ministers

I have already discussed how my ministers are appointed and will therefore not dwell on it. In particular, I pointed out that in some cases, illiteracy is a condition for appointment.

I would like to add simply that it is not fair or honest to accuse my government of corruption, favouritism, nepotism and tribalism. In appointing ministers, I choose people in whom I have trust and confidence.

The rampant talk about rampant corruption is an emanation of the diabolical minds that stir up hate in this country. Once I have appointed a minister, it is his responsibility to ensure the smooth running of his ministry. I do not interfere in their affairs. I cannot run the country and at the same time run ministries or run after ministers. Our ministers are mature and responsible individuals and have full independence to do as they please in the name of the country.

When one listens to the international press and our enemies, one comes away with the feeling that corruption is the order of the day in Mandzah. I recall that one of my ministers tried to smuggle gold bars and diamonds out of the country but was caught at our national airport. Yet everybody says we are all corrupt. How come the customs people arrested the minister?

Wicked minds will respond that, had the minister shared the booty, he would not have been arrested. My government cannot act on hearsay. It is true that the customs people arrested the minister but when I asked him if it was true that he had been trying to smuggle out gold and diamonds, he denied the allegations and said he wasn't smuggling out anything. The gold bars and diamonds found on him were mine that I had given him to take abroad for safekeeping. I challenge anybody to tell me on what grounds the minister should have been prosecuted when he was simply carrying out my instructions.

Last year rumours were rife that the managing director of our Central Bank had fled the country with millions of dollars. If the allegation is true, Kom Mandooh will pay dearly for his life because, prior to his fleeing with the money, I had asked him to transfer $2.3 million to my personal national bank account and he said we didn't have that kind of money. We have sent word out to our foreign friends to help track him down, but we know nothing may come of it because our foreign friends don't usually arrest African nationals who have fled to their countries, especially if they are carrying excess luggage of ill-gotten wealth.

It is not true that ill-gotten gains seldom prosper because when they involve development aid funds, they thrive.

I remember that a few months ago, I contacted my colleague, President Jean-Emile de L'Argent of the Romance Republic, to help us locate Kom Mondooh but he told me point blank that development aid funds are supposed to be ploughed back into the economies of the countries that gave the aid. He said there are many officially accepted ways such as depositing the funds in a bank account abroad, procuring all goods and services from the country that provided the aid, and spending over half of the funds to pay foreign experts, etc. In fact, he said aid is not charity and it was for this and other reasons that all aid donors impose very stringent conditions on the recipient country.

There have been rumours that I have not been able to pay civil servants for a few months because there is no money in our banks since government officials who are indebted to the banks have not been repaying their loans. The same rumours say that the courts cannot do anything about it because those involved are my protégés. I am afraid I cannot intervene in purely financial transactions entered into between banks and individual civil servants. If I intervene, as I usually do, people who have nothing to say will say the executive branch is interfering in the exercise of justice. If I don't, they will say I am protecting my people. Given the dilemma, I have decided to stay out of it.

As everyone knows, a bank is a financial and not a cultural, much less a religious institution. I believe people are getting confused because the differences between banks and religious institutions are being blurred, especially because religious institutions are becoming just as financial as purely financial institutions. Some of our religious people take the tithe that our people pay and live on it far more luxuriously than our financial magnates. They want to imitate the way I and my ministers live on the people's taxes. But they are making a mistake because taxes are economic and financial while tithes are in the religious domain.

Over the past few years, I have personally intervened for our banks to give loans to many of our citizens who would not otherwise be able to compete with the foreign businessmen in our country. Unfortunately, these citizens take the loans and default on the payments. In some cases, instead of using the money for the intended purpose, they use it for non-productive purposes. For example, they fly to Tubab, deposit the money in their foreign accounts, buy cars and are unable to reimburse the loans.

Government has before it draft guidelines proposed eight years ago by the Mandzah Bankers Association on Loans and Loan Repayments. A committee will be established to study the proposals and make recommendations to government. Until that is done, I appeal to everyone to remain calm as government is doing everything possible to encourage our banks to be more pushy in the current international market.

16

Tribalism

One thing I do not understand about the workings of the human mind is the way our people think. As a people, we must transcend petty jealousies and build one strong and united nation. It is not because half the cabinet is made up of people from my ethnic group that I am tribalistic. I have always endeavoured to balance all appointments. For example, since key positions in government, the army and the state-owned enterprises are occupied by people from my ethnic group, I have ensured that the other positions are offered to people from the other ethnic groups. There is something for everybody in this government, and that is why our slogan is "Deeds Not Words".

Some people have complained bitterly about developments in my home village. They look, for example, at the international airport we built there, just 340 km from our national capital, and say I wasted the country's resources. It is not true that an airport is a waste and they know it. To ensure that the airport is fully operational and that its ultra-modern facilities are used, we will gradually divert all international traffic there. This should help relieve the heavy traffic at our present international airport that is lacking in some very elementary facilities.

Besides, since all visiting heads of state to our country must visit my hometown, it was imperative to upgrade the facilities at that airport. Maybe our people do not know that most African heads of state travel in their own private jets. Our airports must therefore be equipped to handle them. I don't see anything tribalistic about an airport.

Again, tongues have been wagging that I have built the most modern schools and colleges in my home town, that I have transferred most ministries to my village, that the highway to my village is the best in the country, in short, that while I am busy developing my home town, I am forgetting about other parts of the country.

Oh that people will be more honest! The same people that are saying all these things forget that I have, as part of my policy to develop all parts of our country, built a presidential mansion and guesthouse in every provincial capital. Since I usually visit each province at least once every four years, it makes a lot of economic sense to build the mansions and guesthouses. Moreover, each provincial headquarters has a fully operational party house, a detachment of our armed forces to suppress dissent, a tight security prison for enemies of our government, a church and mosque, and a presidential ranch where I can retire to with visiting heads of state and have simple, rustic fun. It is true that because I have been very busy, I haven't used most of these facilities for six years, but they nevertheless are part of our country's assets.

I shall nor lend credence to the accusations that my castle in the village is atomic-bomb proof. The truth is that since my village is sitting along an earthquake fault line, the architects whom we hired from Tubab Four, Tubab Seventeen and Tubab Eleven, recommended that we make it earthquake proof. Earth-quake-proof and atomic bomb proof are not the same thing, and people should not go round discrediting me for no reason.

It is true that we maintain a full-time staff of cooks, watchmen, clerks, telephone operators, stewards, janitors, and so on in my castle. It is well known that each time I travel anywhere in Mandzah, I take plane loads and plane loads of people with me, including battalions of our armed forces, the military band, ministers, party luminaries, ambassadors, students and market women to cheer and applaud everything I say. These people have to be housed and fed in line with the elementary law of courtesy and hospitality enshrined in our culture.

17

Political Prisoners and Human Rights

Rebels and dissidents without a cause have made war songs out of the state of our prisons and human rights situation. We are just as interested as they are in condemning the imprisonment of innocent people for their political beliefs and the atrocious conditions under which our prisoners live.

A government is judged by the way in which it treats its citizens. The entire world knows that because we have made the respect for human rights a priority concern, we have been treating our people the way they deserve to be treated.

We are proud that we are one of the very few countries in Africa without political prisoners in the sense of the word. Those with long memories will recall that when I celebrated the 30th anniversary of my coming to power, I released all those who had been held in solitary confinement in our prisons throughout the country. We freed murderers, robbers, traffic violators, drug pushers, and so many other criminals. I even authorized the immediate release of journalists who took the law instead of the pen in their hands to insult me.

We recognize that we still have many other prisoners languishing in our jails, but we believe that they are getting what they bargained for. We may be living in the jungle as our Tubab friends love to assert, but we are guided by the norms of civilized society.

I am not aware of any nation that pardons traitors and spies. Had the planned diabolical actions of some of these people succeeded, this country would have convulsed under the weight of sheer suffering and deprivations because I wouldn't have been around to render the invaluable services that every citizen has come to associate me with. Even the Western world with its gory tales of crimes, does not condone treachery. Anyone who betrays his or her country is not fit to live.

The world's most vicious wars and dictators didn't come from Africa although the Western media is piling insults on us everyday for locking up a few misguided citizens. Where were they when Hitler and his master race were terrorizing the entire world? Hitler was anything but African, and I don't think it is fair for people to confuse Aryan with African.

Let us look at Wuwuslovia where human beings are killing one another while civilized society is going about its business as if nothing is happening just because the poor people do not have oil or a strategic resource. Defenders of human civilization watched with bemused distraction as concentration camps, reminiscent of Hitler's days, were being put up like tents all over the place.

The world's collective memory is too short, and when it comes to Africa, everyone ridicules us for being poor, conveniently forgetting that modern Western economies are built on resources plundered in Third World countries as well as on the blood, sweat and tears of our forebears.

That our prisons abound with traitors is a known fact, and we do not have any reason to apologize to anyone. We cannot pardon criminals who commit massacres against the people. Those who, knowingly and intentionally, betray their country, must face the full force and might of the law.

There can be no worse betrayal of a country than the attempt to assassinate its leader.

We cannot permit our citizens, under the mask of political refugees, to go round the world speaking ill of their duly elected Life-President, and accusing him of all frivolous crimes that cannot be proven. My people are free to criticize government constructively and to make suggestions. But we refuse to award certificates of merit to traitors, liars and rebels.

As President of Mandzah, I am the captain of the ship of state. No matter how buffeted we are by the storms of hate, calumny and treachery, it is my responsibility to steer the ship of state safely to shore. The talk in all quarters about political prisoners and prisoners of conscience in my country is gibberish. We have people in our jails that do not love their country and who spend all their time interfering in the way the country is run.

We have said we are willing to pardon people for their crimes but certainly not for treachery. Anyone who attempts to overthrow me is directly attempting to overthrow the institutions of this country. We shall never permit that to pass.

International doomsayers have been pointing accusing fingers at me for having locked up many opponents since I assumed power. If I had to do it all over, I would not have given them room to live. They deserve a fate worse than death. Traitors are not political prisoners but criminals.

As to the number of traitors we have imprisoned, I say very few. We have about 3,000 from the first fake attempted coup, 1396 from the second one, 6751 from the third one, 34 from the fourth one, 908 from the fifth one and 8794 from the latest real one. All told, this is far less than the number of drug pushers, murderers, armed robbers, etc. in Tubab jails. When people quote statistics, they should know what they are doing.

With regard to the conditions of detention of our traitors, we have said our traitors are treated far better than many prisoners throughout the world. We are so kind that we even give them one meal a day. And unlike many other countries, we do not subject them to slave labour. It is a sad fact of history that the most vociferous nations in the world today, when it comes to championing the cause of political traitors, are the same countries that subjugated our brothers and sisters to the most ignominious barbarism in history. I am referring to the slave trade. The developed countries and so-called civilized world owe their development to the precious blood our people shed on their behalf. Yet they don't want to hear us talk about reparations because it will give them a guilty conscience.

We believe that political sabotage of our statehood is just as reprehensible as the rape and subjugation of our economies. We have decided that instead of forcing our political traitors to work, we will continue to give them the opportunity to learn. We have professors who teach them indoctrination and propaganda so that, if they are lucky to leave prison alive, they will be very useful to their country.

Since prisoners are after all prisoners and not free people, they are held in underground dungeons located in several parts of the country. As part of the punishment to reform them, they are given a daily dose of some of the best modern punishment borrowed freely from Tubab: beatings, blindfolding, keeping them in shackles and chains, electrocution, starvation, etc.

18

Democratization

There has been a lot of noise about the lot of hot air blowing from Tubab East. Everywhere on this continent people are clamouring for multi-party politics as if it is a panacea to the fatally infectious problems that beset us. Traitors, enemies of the people, hooligans and vandals have picked this up and are going round the country lighting the fire of hate in the name of multi-party politics. This country has known party politics in the past, and we know what it did to our people. That's why we abolished it in the first place.

Then the developed world turns round as if it just woke up from slumber to lecture us about the evils of our single national parties which have wrought so much good to our people. Where were they when the people themselves forced me to adopt the single party? Where were they when we abolished freedom of the press, encouraged hero-worship, arrested, tortured and assassinated our opponents, disbanded parliament, diverted national funds to our own use, and so on and so forth? I say where were they? Yet they know that every leader is hostage of his people.

In any case, while in the past I adamantly refused to bow to this passing democratic fad, I must readily admit that we in Africa recognize that we are part of the world. In this communications age, we know that anything that takes place in one country is immediately relayed to the entire world, and that when it concerns Africa, it is drummed up, magnified and blown out of proportion.

Aren't we witnesses to the several conclaves that our developed world pay masters have been holding recently to force us to go democratic or lose their financial support? Of course, this is blackmail because how come it is only now that they see the evil in our one-party system?

When the information that I must go democratic or give up my presidential throne was first relayed to me by the ambassador of one of the Tubab West countries accredited to my country, I couldn't believe my ears. My immediate reaction was that who cares if economic aid is cut off as long as military aid is strengthened? Our armed forces have sacrificed too much for this country. They have quelled every real or imagined rebellion with crude barbarism, and refused to back any of their wayward colleagues who attempted to take over the country by force of arms. Consequently, it is not because we are facing the most difficult economic problems that we should sacrifice people who have already sacrificed their lives to save this country from the tyranny of a few blighted souls.

On account of my sense of proportion, and not willing at any time to take crucial decisions without consulting my advisers and retainers, I sought counsel of my inner circle when this democratization wind started blowing. My closest aides were summoned to my palace and I put the cards on the table. I explained to my ministers, kingmakers and security people that we should cut the grass under the peoples' feet by declaring our open support for the multi-party system of politics. My reasoning was that if we allowed the few self-seeking, self-centred, power-hungry and so-called champions of multi-party politics to form political parties, we would have so many parties that we would win any elections pants down since we are better organized and control not only the press but the life of the citizenry.

My inner circle unanimously vetoed me. The minister of state for security, spying and coups asserted that the army was fully behind me, and assured me of the military's loyalty and continued support in crushing any demonstrations in favour of the multi-party system. He convinced us that, as far as he was concerned, there was no coup in the offing.

For his part, the minister of finance, pre-finance, debts and liquidation insisted that we should call the developed world's bluff because they could not afford to cut off economic aid to us. He referred specifically to the Summit Meeting of Romance-speaking countries that took place in La Taule at which President Littleround had announced to the world, between burps, that his country was now going to champion the cause of democracy in Africa. All of us laughed because, as politicians, we know that public statements don't mean a thing especially as President Littleround and his country have been the greatest supporters of dictatorship in Africa. It is well known in international circles that the only reason the romance Republic can stand up and be counted is that it has colonies and some powerful African leaders supporting it. It is clear that as long as nationals of Romance-speaking African countries don't rise up against their colonial master by rising up against the dictators they support financially and militarily, Romance-speaking Africa will remain in perpetual bondage.

There is no reason to believe that our Tubab friends will abandon those of us tapped by fate to rule over Africa. The number of people dying as a result of our sacrificial services to our colonial masters is still too small to stir the conscience of the world. Furthermore, although the Cold War has ended, my country is still very strategically located and the West uses it as a staging post for countless operations as was the case recently when the Coalition decided to bomb Bedfiri.

Also, we produce the raw materials Tubab countries need badly. My advisers have warned that our party stands to lose support throughout the country if we throw the country to the opposition leaders whose aim is to overthrow my government democratically.

My advisers are adamant that we must not yield to pressure from the street. They, all to a man, have started weeping because they are afraid that everything they have stolen in their life will be taken away from them. Many of them even say they know they will be tried for graft, embezzlement and tribalism, and have pleaded with me not to hearken to the call of multi-party politics.

The businessmen, for their part, sent a delegation to see me because they said if the opposition ever got into power, it would set up a commission of enquiry to look into shady business deals and why they weren't paying taxes. The delegation therefore counseled that I should make it appear that I had been a democrat all along and all would be well. They pointed to our constitution that guaranteed multi-party politics although we opted for a single party since independence.

As it usually happens in my country in such situations, before I realized it, the president of the Pfunam Wing of our party, Hon. Dji Enen, went on the airwaves with a message from the entire Pfunam population pledging their loyalty to me and abusing those in support of multi-party politics as opportunists, rabble rousers, and enemies of mankind as a whole. I cannot say how Hon. Enen, my uncle, was able to mobilize the people so fast, but that is the way he works. His people have so much confidence in him that they have given him the green light to say anything he likes at any time in their name without bothering to consult them. They know he is a representative of valour, and that he will never betray them. Accordingly, Hon. Enen can take to the airwaves at any time to whip up support for me, the party, the government and my family. He does it so well that people just follow him blindly.

Hon. Enen is well known to be a crowd puller. He is the one who organizes the well-known welcome ceremonies for which our country has become famous abroad. He can, at a moment's notice, mobilize hundreds of thousands of people to line the highway from the airport to my residence to show our foreign visitors that my people love me. The foreigners themselves love this because it gives them the sense of worth that they don't have in their own country. Hon. Enen can also commandeer all private and public vehicles unannounced, close down all schools to allow the students to take a glimpse at me and my guest, organize sumptuous champagne-popping ceremonies, etc.

Anyone who knows my country knows that one of the hallmarks of my people is their frankness and honesty. My people will never call a white man black because they know he is white and will never change his spots. My people are not people to say they love me if they don't.

When the stench of multi-party politics drifted from our neighbouring countries and filled the air in Mandzah, the people started rumbling like our volcanic mountain in eruption and I was flooded with messages of support from all segments of the population encouraging me to be steadfast in what I was doing. The minister of information, disinformation, propaganda, and censorship immediately summoned the mass media as well as our single national daily, the *Mandzah Oracle*, to publish nothing else but the messages that were pouring into the People's House. Then all branches of our national party started sending delegations to wish me and the party well. Never before has an entire nation showed such massive support for its esteemed leader.

Credit for the success of the rallies and the goodwill messages must go to Hon. Enen and to the political bureau of our party for engineering such jubilant spontaneous demonstrations of mass support in favour of our single party. Civil servants abandoned their offices for days, including such learned men as doctors, university professors, teachers, and churchmen to pay homage to me and the party. Churchgoers fasted and prayed for my government and me and citizens from all walks of life left their daily chores to march triumphantly, sometimes under heavy downpours and sometimes under the scorching heat, to show their allegiance to me. Not since the fateful events of two years ago when a group of disgruntled intellectuals incited our people to riot, through tracts, has this country seen such an outpouring of love and support for its leader.

Those clamouring to aspire to multi-party politics, something they don't know well because we nipped it in the bud in this country over thirty years ago, felt that they had at last found a cure for our nation's ills. I leave it to them to continue dreaming and scheming.

One significant event occurred early last week in the midst of all this. A group of school dropouts started demonstrating in front of the Tubab One Embassy calling for party politics to flourish in this country. My minister of state security, spying and coups and the head of the intelligence unit assembled a few crack troops and dispersed the crowd with water cannons and tear gas. Before I knew it, the news had spread like our dry season bush fire that destroys everything on its path to other parts of the country. The millions of unemployed youths roaming our streets immediately joined the bandwagon of vagrants and combed the entire country inciting peaceful citizens to rise up and protest against the singly-party system which has brought us so much peace and stability, and rid Mandzah of tribalism.

A crisis committee of our party immediately came up with the ingenious idea that I should proclaim to the world that our party had never really been opposed to multi-party politics and that, while we are not really against it, we want to march towards it gradually on our own steam and without adopting a model that may be incompatible with our way of life.

This is the approach we have decided to adopt. We will continue to proclaim to the world that we have been democrats at heart all along and that our single party is indeed an incarnation of the virtues of democracy and multi-party politics. The world is naïve enough to believe anything that comes out of the mouth of a president.

Part of the marauding band of rabble-rousers calling for democracy to triumph and multi-party politics to flourish was bold enough to say it wanted a national conference. This government does not believe that what the country needs is something reminiscent of the Nuremberg trial. We have seen what happened in other national conferences and are sorry for democracy. Self-proclaimed life-presidents were insulted before the entire world; ministers bared for embezzlement, graft and mismanagement. We say if other people are stupid enough to wash their filthy linen in the full glare of international lights, we in Mandzah are not that stupid.

Was I not the one who decided many years ago that we should allow conflicting ideas to be expressed within our single national party? I did it out of the conviction that since we cannot see ourselves but by reflection, we needed to give the opportunity to our party rank and file to have a voice in the election of their leaders.

This is why the party adopted the list system and then later on approved the idea that there should be many party candidates for any elective office. It is with pride that I report the success of that decision.

The peace and harmony that this country enjoys, the stability of my government in the face of stridently virulent opposition, the great progress we have made in all fields, can all be traced to the effective policies adopted by our party. This is the news that we have been trumpeting and that has somewhat calmed down tempers. We intend to play it by the ear and see how other countries are handling this multi-party virus. We had thought that we could combat it alone, but we realize, regrettably for our people, that it has reached continental proportions that only the heads of state can marshal the support necessary to eradicate it.

Democracy must come by the ballot box when it is well stuffed and not from the street. It is not normal that just slightly over 30 years after we obtained our independence, people should show such impatience in the face of our failures. Many of my colleagues have stumbled and fallen on the road to democracy and I am not going to be one of them. For now we have the army in control and our foreign friends are backing us because they don't trust the opposition. Since the opposition people are too smart, and that's the last quality a white man wants to recognize in a black man, those of us reigning like president-monarchs have a long lease on our political life.

Anyone who has eyes to see should see what is happening in Njindut. My friend, President Job Nemah Mbubam, has almost lost his throne for giving in to the passing democratic fad. Thank God his Western backers, who had initially taken pleasure in lecturing African presidents on the virtues of democracy, have realized that it is better to maintain us in power since we are more gullible and easy to manipulate than to allow the young uncontrollable and unpredictable radicals and rascals to take over.

19

Mandzah and Africa in the World

A number of events have been taking place over the last few years that have completely changed the course of Tubab East history, and thus that of the world. I am referring, of course, to the tumultuous changes taking places in Tubab East and to the establishment of a unified Tubab West market.

Some African intellectuals have been showing concern about what may happen to Africa especially as all the Tubabs seem to want to bury their political differences in favour of forging closer unity and enhancing the opportunities for economic development.

Like all my colleagues, I believe the best thing for us to do is to fold our hands and wait. Our wait-and-see policy has served us well so far and there is no reason to change it. One does not change a winning formula.

We politicians are not overly worried about what our intellectuals claim to see. The world is not and has never been run by intellectuals. Intellectuals should consequently concern themselves with their laboratories or research publications and leave politics to us. We do not meddle in the way they conduct their experiments or write their research and scholarly papers.

We are in close touch with our Tubab friends and there is no cause for alarm. Already, there are unmistakable signs that our close cooperation is bearing fruit. Anyone who has been listening to the pronouncements of our Tubab friends would have realized that all of them are fighting our cause for us. They have told us not to worry that they are more concerned about their own survival than about our own, and I personally do not see why we should be concerned about things that do not concern us. If the Tubabs want greater political and economic unity, I do not see the problem. It will make for greater peace among them. The results of their closer cooperation are showing on the rest of the world.

For example, Tubab West has come together as a family to help their economically beleaguered and politically restive Tubab East cousins in the face of the massive reconstruction that is necessary in Tubab East. We welcome this as an improvement in the international political and economic climate all the more as, since independence, Tubab West has persistently and consistently refused to help Africans in the reconstruction of their economies.

Furthermore, our export crops will continue to be sold at depressingly low prices, but out of the generosity of the Tubab's heart, we shall gain in terms of more food aid and underdevelopment assistance. The Tubabs will continue to discourage Africans from embarking on the road to manufacturing finished or semi-finished goods because they will claim that our products won't be competitive on the Tubab market. It will therefore make real economic sense for us to be eternally dependent on them for everything we need. They will establish a few industries in Mandzah to run away from high labour costs and pollution at home. In return, we will close down our own industries to avoid open competition with theirs. The money so saved will be used to purchase Tubab products and thus develop all sectors of their economy. They will be seen as strong producers and we will be seen as avid consumers. This is what is known in economics as division of labour. One of its major advantages is economies of scale.

On the political front, we the leaders of Africa must continue to show solidarity with our colonial parents because we are nothing without them. They have made us in their own image and it is this beautiful image that the opposition wants to tarnish by portraying us as good-for-nothing leaders because our countries owe their present state of advanced underdevelopment to us.

I would like to refer to just two simple examples in recent times that confirm why African leaders must cling to the tails of their colonial parents if they want to continue enjoying power.

The entire world knows that President Pual Fraudulence Yabi of the Lions Republic is my friend, and that sometimes some of our colonial parents go through me to contact him. We all know that he was recently trounced in his country's first ever-democratic elections decried by all international observers as the most fraudulent elections anywhere in Africa. All the same, with the full military and economic support of President Littleround of the Romance Republic, President Yabi categorically refused to concede defeat and instead declared a state of emergency in his country, dumped the opposition people in jail, and left the country to visit his castles and clinic and, presumably, to consult with his financial doctors in Jeniva about the state of his personal national accounts.

The Romance Republic, everyone knows, is afraid that if she should allow real democracy to triumph in Africa, she would lose her colonial empire and lucrative markets. This explains why she has continued to prop up crumbling dictatorships in Africa instead of sustaining the democratic momentum that has gathered speed today on the continent.

Those of us still lucky to be in power know that we will be forced by events and circumstances to organize so-called democratic elections. Knowing that our people are sick and tired of us, it is certain that if we play the game by the rules laid down by our Tubab parents, no opposition party, no matter how strong and popular, will dislodge us.

There is also the case of the United Tribes Organization (UTO) that is supposed to be an emanation of the political will of all the tribes in the world. The United Conquerors Republic, with its allies and coalition partners, has taken it over and is using it to foster its vital interests and to dominate the Third World. When they believe their interests are threatened by a so-called Third World country, they instruct the UTO to condemn the accused country and to impose sanctions on it, and then take it upon themselves to exact compliance with the UTO's sanctions by attacking the country militarily in the name of the UTO. The world has watched in submissive awe as the Tubab coalition, the brotherhood of colour, launched devastating attacks on some of our colleagues for the simple reason that we are neither supposed to be heard nor seen. Since our survival as leaders depends to a large extent on our doing their will, we have had to applaud and celebrate each time a bomb fell somewhere in the Third World killing people and damaging property.

Nevertheless, as leaders, we must be cautious in our dealings with our Tubab parents. We can continue to kill a few opposition people and lock up demonstrators as well as to muzzle the press. As long as the numbers are not too high, our Tubab parents will not bat an eye. However, while Tubabs, especially the Romance Republic, the United Conquerors Republic, Hegemony and Criton, have a great sense of duty of their mission to defend human civilization, we should not push our luck too far. If we kill just the right number of our people so that there is no widespread public outcry, Tubabs and the white world at large will not stir.

We must at all times remember that Tubabs owe the land they occupy to conquest and that they have, throughout their own history, been through wars, pogroms, assassinations, concentration camps, ethnic purification, etc. Thus, as far as they are concerned, what we are doing today is no big deal, especially as Africa is too far away for them to hear the anguished screams of the few people we slaughter from time to time.

20

My Legacy

In the thousands of interviews that I have accorded the press in all the countries I have visited throughout the world, the one question that is usually on the lips of journalists is what I would like to leave the world as my legacy. I have always had a pat response, and that is that I will not let history be the judge.

But then seriously speaking, I think it is offensive, while there is no sign that I am dying or that I intend to relinquish power, to ask me what I hope to leave to history. History is rich enough and does not need anything from me although I'd like to thank those who believe that history is not history without me.

It is very premature for me to carve for myself a place in history while I am still alive. I do not want to be like my Tubab colleagues who are always worrying about what the world will say about them after they are gone. After they are gone, they are gone.

I should like to point out, however, that I am not in the same league as my Tubab colleagues. For one thing, as a duly elected Life-President and President-monarch, I have all the time in the world to prepare my legacy and to die if I want. After all, since no other president will come after me, nothing will be interred with me.

Furthermore, this is just Part One of Born to Rule. There will be more parts to leave our people in the fullness of time. But then since I pledged openness, I might as well give a glimpse to the world of what my legacy might be.

I have ruled Mandzah for over 30 years, and according to our constitution, I am a Life-President. This, I think, is the greatest legacy anyone can ever leave his people.

I shall also leave behind a politically mature people who refused to walk in the shadow of sycophants, traitors and dissidents. It is to the foresight and sound judgment of my people that they lifted me to the loftiest position in Mandzah.

For the moment, I am Life-President, Commander-in-Chief of the Armed Forces, National President of the Mandzah National Union Party, Chancellor of the National University, Keeper of the Till, Custodian of National Wisdom, Depository of Talent, Most Exemplary Paramount Chief, and so many other titles.

Since, according to our traditions, it is the people who take gifts to the chief, I am sure that my people reserve me more titles while I reserve for them more surprises.

21

Post Scriptum

Just as this historical treatise was being finalized, I had to page my publisher all over the place, including his favourite palm wine drinking houses to inform the reader about the latest mission I have successfully accomplished.

My vigilant security people have just announced the crushing of an attempted insurrection by a group of misguided soldiers who think they can take the law into their hands, overthrow me and govern our people better. I am sure it was much relief to my people when we reversed the situation and I went on the air to announce that I was still in full command and in charge.

My government has given firm instructions to our security staff to arrest all those involved and their relatives, friends, colleagues, acquaintances, and anyone who knows them even remotely. I have also declared a state of emergency. There will be a dusk to dawn curfew and all political parties are requested, in their own interest and for their own security, to suspend any planned meetings or rallies.

The reports coming in are still sketchy, but I promise to report on the situation fully in the next volume of Born to Rule. Already, as has always been the case in the past, we have started receiving massages of support from the people, beginning with members of parliament, the civil service union, trade unions, market women, the business community, foreign diplomats, religious leaders, students, the armed forces, foreign residents, etc. Nevertheless, before the world press starts making its money on our backs because of this minor incident, we would have executed all the rebels and their supporters. Amnesia International, as far as we know, does not have, has never had, and will never have the capacity to resurrect people from the dead.

www.ingramcontent.com/pod-product-compliance
Lightning Source LLC
Chambersburg PA
CBHW011744290426
44113CB00017BA/2648